M000281954

"Our thoughts have the power to help or hurt us. So what do we do when our thoughts leave us feeling beaten, bruised, and out of control? In *Transforming Your Thought Life*, Sarah reminds us that the answer lies not inside ourselves but within the pages of Scripture. Read this book now!"

—**Lauren Gaskill,** author of *Into the Deep* and president of She Found Joy

"Our minds are busy places, and often they're filled with harmful thoughts and motives. In *Transforming Your Thought Life*, Sarah returns meditation to its rightful place in the Christian life, teaching us to leverage the power of Scripture to shape our thoughts. Sarah's vulnerable personal applications and fresh perspectives challenge me to clean up the playground of my mind!"

—**Amy Carroll,** speaker and writer for Proverbs 31 Ministries and author of *Breaking Up with Perfect* and *Exhale*

"With honesty and transparency, Sarah shows us the power of God's Word and its ability to conquer and destroy the unwanted, harmful thoughts that frequent our minds. Sarah not only points us to the solution but she also takes us by the hand and guides us step-by-step through the process of building lasting habits to experience victory through Christ."

—**Kate Motaung,** author of *A Place to Land: A Story of Longing and Belonging*

"Changing the way we think so that we can live a more joyful and victorious life sounds great, but it seems daunting. In *Transforming Your Thought Life*, Sarah Geringer doesn't just tell us what it looks like to experience change through Christian meditation. She shows us *how* to change the way we think . . . every step of the way."

—**Lynn Cowell,** author of *Make Your Move* and member of the Proverbs 31 Ministries writing and speaking team

"This book is practical, accessible, and potentially life-changing. Sarah Geringer has much to offer any woman who wishes she could put a harness on her own runaway thoughts."

—**Christie Purifoy,** author of *Roots and Sky* and *Placemaker*

"In this book, Sarah dispels the myths behind Christian meditation and introduces us to its many benefits. She masterfully invites us into the presence of God with meditations that satisfy the deep needs of our souls. Through *Transforming Your Thought Life*, discover afresh that God's Word truly is the answer to all of our problems and that meditating on his Word transforms our hearts and minds, equipping us to face any challenge by his grace."

—**Denise Pass,** speaker, worship leader, and author of *Shame Off You* and *31 Days to Hope Reinvented*

"When Sarah Geringer writes about meditation, she isn't just talking about the thoughts we think. She weaves together the depths of her own life experience, the richness of Scripture, and the fruits of her own contemplation into a beautiful tapestry. The unique gift of this book is how you can read it chapter by chapter or choose the chapter that fits your own thought life at that moment. Either way, it will guide you into grace."

—**Travis Scholl,** author of *Walking the Labyrinth*

"*Transforming Your Thought Life* is a valuable resource for every believer. In this comprehensive book, Sarah dives head-first into harnessing our thoughts with the life-giving practice of meditating on God's Word. Sharing many of her own struggles and stories, Sarah tackles challenges from her life with authenticity and courage. Her candid stories draw us in, helping us to see our own struggles as we recognize our need to filter our thoughts through Scripture. Sarah guides us closer to God, demonstrating how Christian meditation can transform our thoughts and heal our wounds."

—**Ginger Harrington,** author of *Holy in the Moment*

"Sarah Geringer knows this to be true: our only hope for true transformation in this life is through the Word of God. With joy and honesty, she beckons us to meditate daily on a Bible passage and guides us in understanding all the whys, hows, and whats of Christian meditation. What a gift! Sarah's methods can make all the difference in our daily thought struggles. I am a new meditation fan and recommend this book for personal and group studies alike!"

—**Maria Furlough,** author of *Confident Moms, Confident Daughters* and *Breaking the Fear Cycle*

"If you think meditation isn't for Christians, think again. Sarah Geringer deftly grounds her meditative practices in Scripture alongside compelling personal stories and practical, accessible advice. In *Transforming Your Thought Life*, Sarah shows us a path through daily anxieties, distractions, and negative thoughts toward healing, peace, and wholeness. This book is a must-read for anyone yearning to transform negative thought patterns in order to live more fully in intimate union with God."

—**Michelle DeRusha,** author of *True You*

Transforming
YOUR
Thought Life

Transforming YOUR Thought Life

CHRISTIAN
MEDITATION
IN FOCUS

SARAH GERINGER

LEAFWOOD
P U B L I S H E R S
an imprint of Abilene Christian University Press

TRANSFORMING YOUR THOUGHT LIFE

Christian Meditation in Focus

L E A F W O O D
P U B L I S H E R S
an imprint of Abilene Christian University Press

Copyright © 2019 by Sarah Geringer

ISBN 978-1-68426-210-6 | LCCN 2019013412

Printed in the United States of America

Published in association with WordWise Media Services, 4083 Avenue L, Suite 255, Lancaster, CA 93536.

LIBRARY OF CONGRESS CATALOGING-IN-PUBLICATION DATA
Names: Geringer, Sarah, 1977- author.
Title: Transforming your thought life : Christian meditation in focus / Sarah Geringer.
Description: Abilene, Texas : Leafwood Publishers, 2019.
Identifiers: LCCN 2019013412 | ISBN 9781684262106 (pbk.)
Subjects: LCSH: Thought and thinking—Religious aspects—Christianity. | Meditation—Christianity.
Classification: LCC BV4598.4 .G47 2019 | DDC 248.3/4—dc23
LC record available at https://lccn.loc.gov/2019013412

Cover design by ThinkPen Design
Interior text design by Sandy Armstrong, Strong Design

Leafwood Publishers is an imprint of Abilene Christian University Press
ACU Box 29138
Abilene, Texas 79699

1-877-816-4455
www.leafwoodpublishers.com

19 20 21 22 23 24 / 7 6 5 4 3 2

In memory of my grandparents
Robert, Martina, and Byron
and in honor of Darlene,
whose legacy of faith
blesses me every day.

CONTENTS

ACKNOWLEDGMENTS

I thank God the Father for providing this publishing opportunity for me. He planted a dream inside my heart when I was young, and I praise him for watering and nurturing the seed of that dream even in my years of obscurity. Now I am blessed to share its fruit with the church at large.

I thank Jesus for walking beside me in this writing process. He wrapped me in his loving embrace during the spiritual attacks and talked to me like a friend. His encouragement kept me pushing through the challenges, and I discovered a new love for him while writing this book.

I thank the Holy Spirit for weaving together so many threads along my journey to be published. He brought myriad scriptures to mind while I was writing, directing me along exciting paths for his glory. I am grateful for his creative inspiration.

I thank my husband, Derrick, and children, Drake, Ethan, and Lauren, for persevering with me on my writing journey. Thank you for loving me even when I had "book brain" so many times in the summer of 2018. Every day I thank God that you help make my writing life possible with your understanding and support.

Thanks to my dedicated team who faithfully prayed me through the writing and publishing process. Special thanks to Katie Blackwell, Linda Geringer, Elizabeth Giertz, Rebecca Hastings, Kim Jolly, Cheryl Lutz, Charla Matthews, Rose McCauley, Angel Pennyman, Alyson Perrin, Debbie Putman, Cheryl Reinagel, Lauren Sparks, Karen Smith, Julie Stoller, Vicki Stone, Magdalene Vogel, Meghan Weyerbacher, Kristi Woods, and a few anonymous friends who read my emails and lifted them up to the Lord. I could feel you praying for me!

Thanks to my friends Elaine Goddard, Terri Hutchinson, Gena McCown, Leslie Newman, Denise Ray, and Beth Steffaniak, who also serve as prayer warriors and special supporters. I praise God for crossing our paths at She Speaks and consider you my treasured kindred spirits.

Thanks goes to Christine Becker and Christine Warren, my high school English teachers, who have continually offered support. Every time I saw you in the grocery store or at a downtown art opening, I received your words of affirmation that encouraged me to keep writing. You both have had a powerful impact on my life, and I thank God for you.

Thanks to Elizabeth Krieser for helping me sift through many stories and serving as a lay counselor. I am grateful for our more than thirty years of friendship and look forward to having many more rich conversations with you.

Thanks to Angie Schupp, my ray-of-sunshine friend. Your honesty and belief in my calling as a writer have lifted me up through this journey. I'm so thankful that I get to see you often through BSF.

Thanks to my many blogging friends who offer advice, encouragement, and support. I love you all like family, and I truly hope to meet each one of you in person someday!

Thanks to my local writing guild friends. You have cheered me on for years, and I have learned so much from you. Here's to many more years of lively meetings and laughter.

Thanks to the team at Leafwood Publishers for guiding me along with grace and expertise. I am honored to publish this book with your imprint.

Thanks to my agent, Michelle S. Lazurek. This book would not exist without your wisdom, insight, and hard work. I am looking forward to more collaboration with you, friend.

All glory and praise be to the Lord God Almighty!

HOW CHRISTIAN MEDITATION TRANSFORMS YOUR THOUGHTS

I rejoice in following your statutes as one who rejoices in great riches. I meditate on your precepts and consider your ways. I delight in your decrees; I will not neglect your word.

—PSALM 119:14–16

I stared at the checkbook register. My heartbeat accelerated with anxiety, and my eyes filled with tears. Only $800 in the account to pay $2,000 in bills by the end of the month, and we were only in the middle of October . It was 2007, and I had just found out I was pregnant with our third child. My one-year-old was napping while my three-year-old was watching a *Curious George* episode. How would we weather this challenge?

A few months before, my husband had left his job in the construction industry to be a teacher, which had been his long-held dream. To provide for our family on half his previous salary, he built spec houses on the weekends. My job as an event planner provided a modest income for occasional expenses. Basically, we were living paycheck to paycheck with another baby on the way.

My husband's beautiful spec house had stood vacant for months. We desperately needed that house to sell, or we'd be falling into the debt pit again.

When my husband and I got married in November 2000, we were broke college seniors living in his buddy's basement. The day after our wedding reception, we spread out all our credit cards on the kitchen table and totaled up our debt. We had $25,000 in credit card debt and $40,000 in student loans. The multicolored cards covered the table like a blanket, mocking us with shame and defeat before our careers even began.

It had taken seven years of scrimping to pay off those debts. Seven years of staycations, secondhand clothing, and struggles. Eating Hamburger Helper and renting DVDs from Blockbuster instead of going out with friends. Cloth diapers, thrift stores, hand-me-down furniture, and blizzards of coupons. We had just gotten our heads above water.

That October afternoon, I was standing on the edge of the debt pit again. Trying to distract myself from rising fear, I watched the wild birds pecking at sunflower seeds on the deck. Would I be able to afford seeds to feed them anymore? I wasn't willing to charge birdseed to a line of credit. I didn't want to charge *anything*. But what choice did I have? I needed to pay our bills that very day.

Jesus's words from that morning's Bible Study Fellowship lesson came back to me:

> Therefore I tell you, do not worry about your life, what
> you will eat or drink; or about your body, what you
> will wear. Is not life more than food, and the body
> more than clothes? Look at the birds of the air; they do
> not sow or reap or store away in barns, and yet your
> heavenly Father feeds them. Are you not much more
> valuable than they? (Matt. 6:25–26)

I heard God asking me, "Do you really believe my words are true?"

I studied the birds closely while I considered Jesus's words. The birds' carefree nature was evident, even though I knew their lives weren't easy. They had no homes, pantries, or closets, but their needs were completely met. In ways I could not see, God kept them safe, warm, and dry. He gave them strength and intuition to find food, water, and shelter. He did not forget them or forsake them, and I had to trust that he would not forget or forsake me either. The birds' peaceful *peck, peck, pecks* on the wooden deck rapped on my heart's door.

I wrote out these verses on a page of my mini-notebook:

> So do not worry, saying, "What shall we eat?" or "What
> shall we drink?" or "What shall we wear?" For the
> pagans run after all these things, and your heavenly
> Father knows that you need them. But seek first his
> kingdom and his righteousness, and all these things will
> be given to you as well. Therefore do not worry about
> tomorrow, for tomorrow will worry about itself. Each
> day has enough trouble of its own. (Matt. 6:31–34)

With hands trembling in tentative faith, I called my three-year-old son to pray with me. As I gathered him on my lap, I told him we needed someone to buy the spec house, so we would have money to buy food and clothing as the verses described. We prayed aloud that God would provide for us, just as he provided for the birds on our deck. A sense of peace settled over me after praying these verses with my son.

I placed that little notebook page in my kitchen windowsill, and for the next several days I repeated those verses aloud when I washed my hands or did the dishes. My prayers went up as I spoke the verses, and I told God I was trusting him to provide, as he had promised. When anxiety rose up, I felt centered when I thought about Matthew 6:33: "Seek first the kingdom of God and his righteousness, and all these things will be added to you" (ESV).

In late October, we found a buyer for the spec house at just the right time. I praised God for his timely provision, and I never forgot that powerful lesson.

I didn't realize it at the time, but I was meditating on God's Word. Daily meditation fixed my mind on God's power when I felt anxious, and I experienced his perfect peace when I mulled over Scripture. I learned to apply those verses again and again, especially when the recession rocked our finances again the very next year.

THE DEFINITION OF CHRISTIAN MEDITATION

You may be skeptical about the word *meditation* because of its association with New Age and Eastern religions. I can understand if you feel hesitant, but I'd like to reassure you that the idea of meditation is not foreign to Christianity. It is simply the practice of thinking about Scripture and communing with God. I think you will find it to be a powerful tool for increasing peace in your life.

The word *meditate* is used up to twenty times in the Old Testament, depending on the translation. In Hebrew, the terms *hagah* and *siach* are the primary words used to describe meditation.

Let's look at the original meanings of these terms to understand what meditation means for Christians.

The Hebrew term *hagah* is used in Isaiah 31:4 to describe a lion who "growls" over its prey. The lion growls though bands of shepherds circle around it and try to frighten it with shouts and loud noises. It is undeterred from its focus. Isaiah also uses *hagah* to compare the way mourning doves "moan" to the times King Hezekiah cried out for God's help during a life-threatening illness (Isa. 38:14).

The lion growls because it is centered on its purpose to devour prey. The dove's cry is instinctual and repetitive, basic to its calling as a bird in God's world. Our meditation times may or may not be vocalized. But they can be centered, focused, natural, and repetitive like the animal sounds that inspired Isaiah to use them as metaphors. Our experience of Christian meditation becomes more intentional with memory and practice.

The other main word for meditation in Hebrew is *siach*. It is used to describe concentrated and undistracted thinking in many verses of the Psalms. In Psalm 119, the psalmist uses *siach* eight different times regarding meditating on God's laws and precepts all day long, even into the night (119:15, 23, 27, 48, 78, 97, 99, 148). Sometimes, *siach* is associated with deep feelings of complaint or anguish, as in Psalm 142:2 and Proverbs 23:29. Our times of meditation are not only mental exercises; they are also an invitation to share our hearts with God as we focus on him and cry out to him in honesty.

Christian meditation is neither cold and distant nor fuzzy and nebulous. It involves the solid truth of God's Word, plus our thoughts, feelings, and experiences. It's an invitation to deeper relationship with the One who perfectly loves us. When we make God's character, laws, promises, and works our focus, we engage in Christian meditation.

THE BENEFITS OF CHRISTIAN MEDITATION

Christian meditation is an excellent way to transform your thoughts. You have an average of 60,000 thoughts every day, and up to 80 percent of those thoughts are negative. Almost all of today's negative thoughts are recycled from yesterday's negative thoughts.[1] To stop this negative cycle, you must replace your negative thoughts with positive thoughts rooted in God's Word.

Along with prayer and memorization, meditation can give you the peace you are seeking in your struggles. It has given me peace in financial struggles, marriage strife, extended family issues, career crises, parenting frustrations, and my endless temptation toward self-condemnation. Meditating on Scripture has transformed my thinking, and it has also transformed other areas of my life.

Here are the specific benefits Christian meditation provides.

SPIRITUAL BENEFITS

If you have ever read the story of Job in the Old Testament, you know that your mind is a battlefield between God and Satan, our spiritual enemy. By meditating on Scripture, you can fight the battle where it starts. Since I started meditating, I can now recognize spiritual attacks more quickly. Meditation draws you closer to God and teaches you about his ways, which strengthens your resolve when spiritual battles occur. Richard Foster writes, "What happens in meditation is that we create the emotional and spiritual space which allows Christ to construct an inner sanctuary in the heart."[2] It also gives you peace that passes all understanding even in the middle of your trials.

MENTAL BENEFITS

Meditation is proven to improve your memory skills and increase your concentration.[3] You hide God's Word in your heart during meditation, which means you can pull it out again anytime you need it. Meditating on Scripture also builds your Bible knowledge base. Even though we are blessed to live in an age when the Bible is readily accessible, many of us still don't know God's Word. I have used daily meditation to increase my understanding of the Bible one verse at a time. It's best to first go to an actual Bible to study the verse in its original context, and then to supplement the study with commentaries.

PHYSICAL BENEFITS

Research shows that regular meditation can lower your blood pressure to the point that you may no longer need blood pressure medication.[4] It also reduces the level of cortisol in your body. Cortisol is a stress hormone that causes you to feel hungrier and gain weight—you may be able to shed a few pounds through Christian meditation. Your immune system is boosted when cortisol levels are lowered. I have frequent immune system disruptions, and meditating reduces my stress and my symptoms. I meditate on Bible verses when dealing with insomnia, and it gives me more peaceful sleep.

EMOTIONAL BENEFITS

Contemplating verses about God's love for you can improve your self-image. Meditation can heal your emotional wounds and calm your mood swings. Many of us have scars from the past that serve as sources for our negative thoughts. I have endured a difficult childhood and a challenging marriage. Contemplating the truths in God's Word has helped me heal from many hurts. Every time you are triggered to think in a negative way, you can meditate on Scripture to change your perspective. Over time, you'll learn how to squash those thoughts that stir up negative emotions with the truth of God's Word.

SOCIAL BENEFITS

As you meditate on the kind of life God wants you to live, meditation will empower you to be a better wife, mother, friend, relative, and worker. Self-control is one of the fruits of the Spirit (Gal. 5:22–23), and meditation is a way to practice self-control. When you are tempted to react rather than respond in social situations, Christian meditation can provide the self-control that you need. You will be better prepared in tricky social scenarios with an arsenal of verses tucked away in your mind through meditation. Since I'm a sensitive person who can be slow to respond in social situations, having God's Word as my internal shield has given me the confidence I formerly lacked.

SHARING BENEFITS

When you have God's Word at the ready in your heart, you will no longer be at a loss for words when someone asks you about your faith. Christian meditation helps you have an answer prepared in advance for evangelistic opportunities. I may not share Bible verses with people on the spot, but the truths of the verses are sprinkled through my conversations with strangers, like the salt Jesus calls us to share.

HOW TO PRACTICE CHRISTIAN MEDITATION

Christian meditation is not complicated, time-consuming, or expensive. But you will get the maximum benefits from Christian meditation if you follow these guidelines:

Make it a habit. Choose a time in your daily schedule that you and God can share alone. A few quiet minutes are enough. You can meditate in the shower, during your commute, on your lunch break, while performing chores, during exercise, or right before you go to sleep. As long as meditation is a can't-miss priority on your daily to-do list, it doesn't matter where or when it happens.

Every morning, I choose one verse from my One Year Bible reading and reflect on it throughout the day.

Choose a quiet spot. Your mind itself will try to distract you while you're meditating, so you need to remove sensory distractions from your meditation space. Earplugs or headphones can help in your office or on your commute. A closet or bathroom may be an ideal place to meditate if you are a stay-at-home mom. If you are visually stimulated like I am, go to a place with as little eye candy as possible. I prefer meditating in my bedroom, where I feel the most relaxed and least distracted.

Bring your Bible. Whether you prefer a printed Bible, a Bible app, or a verse written on a sticky note, Scripture needs to be the central point of your meditation time. You can search a regular or online concordance for a topic and meditate on several verses on a certain theme. You could pick one verse from Psalms or Proverbs every day for meditation. You may also enjoy picking verses from the Gospels or New Testament letters. The possibilities are endless, as long as a Bible passage is in place.

Start with prayer. Before meditating, ask God to settle your mind and spirit so you can focus. Ask him to grant you wisdom and application from the section of Scripture. I'm amazed at what the Holy Spirit reveals to me, even in familiar passages, when I pray first!

Repeat the words. Speak the verse slowly several times, pausing on different words each time for different emphasis. Try to consider the meaning of each word as you say it, which will help you gain the maximum benefit from the verse.

Ask questions. Three helpful questions can help you understand the verse even more. Ask (1) What does this verse tell me about God's character? (2) What does this verse tell me about God's master plan? (3) How can I apply this verse to my current situation? These questions help me look at a verse from several vantage points in only a few minutes.

Write it out. Writing your meditation verse helps you commit it to memory. Studies show that when we write something down, we have a significant increase in memory retention compared to typing on a keyboard or tablet.[5] Keep a special notebook in which you simply write out one verse every day. You may be surprised at how much sticking power the verse will have with this technique.

Take notes. Your meditation times may be filled with inspiration and new insights. Don't let them slip by without recording them in a notebook. Review your meditation notes frequently and praise God for what he is showing you in his Word. While writing this book, I'm going back through my journals to harvest material from what I previously learned about God's Word. I didn't know at the time I'd use my notes to write a book someday. Who knows how God will use your notes in the future?

End with prayer. Thank God for what he has revealed to you through the verse. Praise him for any character attributes you discovered in the verse and ask him to help you apply the truth of the verse to your situation. You can also ask him to reveal to you another person with whom you can share the verse.

Post your verse. To help you remember your verse, post it somewhere you will see it often. Jot it on a sticky note and place it on your bathroom mirror, refrigerator door, or computer screen. You can also make the verse a screensaver on your phone or desktop. If you like to keep a daily planner, write it at the top of your daily section. All these methods will help you hide God's Word in your heart and make it more accessible in your memory bank.

Now that you know the basics of Christian meditation, you're ready to get started on this thought transformation journey. In the following chapters, we will look at common problem areas in women's thought lives. We will look at specific verses you can use to decrease your frustration, take control of your thoughts, and increase your peace.

I will share many Bible verses for your benefit. If you're anything like me, you sometimes read verses quickly and skip to the commentary. I encourage you to do something different with this book. Every time you see a Bible verse listed, read it at least three times in a row to start training your mind in the habit of Christian meditation. God's Word has far more power than my words ever will. His Word is living and able to permanently change your thinking like nothing else can. Don't let its power pass by you, friend. Allow it to sink deep into your teachable heart.

Prayer

Father in heaven,

Because you are holy, I want to honor you with my thoughts. My mind belongs to you. I want my thoughts to look more like yours, starting today.

I confess that my thoughts are often a mess. Too many times, my thoughts are stuck in the mud and muck of this world. Sometimes they are fixed on the ghosts of the past when you are calling me forward. My thoughts are often fear-focused rather than joy-focused. I can't change my thoughts myself, Lord. I need your help. Transform me from the inside out.

Thank you for leading me on this journey. I am thankful that the Holy Spirit lives in me and that you will help me persevere through the coming changes.

Please guide me in the days ahead. Remind me to schedule time every day to meditate on your Word. I ask for courage and strength to win the war against my negative thoughts. Give me the mind of Christ as I start on this path of transformation.

In Jesus's name,
Amen.

REFLECTION QUESTIONS

1. What new concept did you learn about Christian meditation in this chapter?

2. Which area of your life—spiritual, mental, emotional, physical, social, or otherwise—could benefit the most from Christian meditation?

3. What is the best time of day for you to use for Christian meditation?

NOTES

[1] Tracie Miles, *Unsinkable Faith: God-Filled Strategies to Transform the Way You Think, Feel, and Live* (Colorado Springs: David C. Cook, 2017), 40.

[2] Richard J. Foster, *Celebration of Discipline: The Path to Spiritual Growth* (San Francisco: Harper San Francisco, 1998), 20.

[3] Emma M. Seppälä, "20 Scientific Reasons to Start Meditating Today," *Psychology Today* (blog), September 11, 2013, https://www.psychologytoday .com/us/blog/feeling-it/201309/20-scientific-reasons-start-meditating-today.

[4] Kristine Crane, "8 Ways Meditation Can Improve Your Life," *Huffington Post* September 9, 2014, https://www.huffingtonpost.com/2014/09/19 /meditation-benefits_n_5842870.html.

[5] Erin Wildermuth, "The Science of Putting Pen to Paper: Studies Show It Forces You to Focus," *Michael Hyatt* (blog), April 10, 2018, https://michaelhyatt .com/science-of-pen-and-paper/.

CHAPTER ONE

CARELESS THOUGHTS

We take captive every thought
to make it obedient to Christ.

—2 CORINTHIANS 10:5

When I'm doing something simple, like driving to pick up my children from school, my unchecked thoughts are often like wild monkeys, shrieking while they jump from branch to branch.

I might start with thinking about weekend plans, then alight on a random memory from grade school, then nurse a grudge about someone I haven't seen in six years. Halfway through my task, I'll wake from a jumbled thought fog and think, "How did I get here?!?"

Women are experts at jumping from topic to topic. It's a God-given gift we have in making meaningful connections. Authors Bill and Pam Farrel describe the working of women's brains as being like spaghetti noodles, twisted and looped all around one another. They write, "Every thought and issue is connected to every other thought and issue in some way. Life is much more of a process for women than it is for men."[1]

By the way, they describe men's thinking like little boxes in waffles. Sometimes I wish my wild-monkey/spaghetti mind worked more like that!

One of our greatest gifts has a dark side. Our spiraling, swirling thoughts can often end up in bad places. If you didn't already know this, I doubt you would be reading this book.

If my thoughts were visible and I had a magnifying glass to peer into my brain, I'd probably find my careless thoughts also look like a junk drawer, crammed with every imaginable thing from various sources.

I just opened my real-life junk drawer. Its primary function is to hold pens and pencils, where many dozens reside. But other flotsam and jetsam from the past two decades have ended up in the drawer too. Here's what I found:

- A light switch for the wall
- An unsheathed razor blade
- A long distance calling card, circa 2002
- Several keys to who knows what
- A tube of lip balm that's missing a lid . . . into the trash it goes!
- Microcassettes for a voice recorder I used during college lectures
- A jewel-shaped, ten-sided die for some board game
- Replacement plastic flowers for my hummingbird feeder

These items represent many of my unexamined thoughts. Some thoughts are out of place, like the light switch. Some are downright dangerous, like the razor blade. Some have outlived their purpose, like the calling card. Some thoughts are disgusting, like the lip balm.

Why don't we tend to our thought lives? It's because they aren't seen by anyone else, same as the junk drawer. We keep hiding messy thoughts away because we think they don't matter.

We undervalue the importance of our thoughts. Our focus turns to our problems without realizing the roots of those problems exist in our ways of thinking. Our thoughts turn into actions, whether good or bad. When the majority of our thoughts are negative, our quality of life suffers.

Have you ever quit a job that you hated? I did that not so long ago. When I moved away from that toxic situation, I realized how much it had affected my thinking. Months after I left, my thoughts would be riding a furious, bitter train in random moments. I was shocked to discover the strong grip that negative environment still had on my mind, and I had to meditate on God's Word to put those thoughts to rest.

Stepping back and examining your thoughts is called *meta-cognition,* or thinking about thinking. In the beginning of this thought-life transformation process, we'll think about all kinds of thoughts. The overarching description of these thoughts is *careless*, or *unexamined*. To have victory in your thought life, you must think about the quality of your thoughts.

TRANSFORMATION IS A FIGHT

I need to warn you—this transformation isn't going to be easy. You'll be fighting yourself and an unseen enemy. You may even be fighting others in this battle.

FIGHTING YOURSELF

If you've ever started an exercise or diet program, you know how difficult it is to persist in a new, healthy habit. Your flesh seems to war against you. I remember doing the cabbage soup diet in college, which lasted about three days. On the fourth morning, I caved and ate a chocolate chip granola bar instead of soup for breakfast. No other granola bar had ever tasted so good! My flesh was crying out for carbs, and the perfectly healthy cabbage soup got tossed.

Jesus tells us in Matthew 26:41, "The spirit is willing, but the flesh is weak." Paul describes the war between his flesh and his spirit in Romans 7:15–25. Your thought-life struggle is real, and you are your own worst enemy.

Nothing strengthens your mind more than meditating on Scripture. God's Word will cover your thoughts like a shield. If you're fighting poor thoughts, you can cry out to God for help in this process. He will strengthen you with custom-fit verses for your battles.

FIGHTING YOUR ENEMY

As soon as Satan finds out you are starting on a journey toward thought-life transformation, expect a battle. Your mind is the main place where the enemy and his cohorts wage war against you. Ephesians 6:12 describes our battle like this: "For we are not fighting against flesh-and-blood enemies, but against evil rulers and authorities of the unseen world, against mighty powers in this dark world, and against evil spirits in the heavenly places" (NLT).

Satan slings ugly, hateful, doubtful, unforgiving, and condemning arrows into your mind's battlefield. The flames of those arrows alight on the tinder of your unexamined thoughts and catch fire, which instantly blazes through your camp.

If you've ever had a problem that you just couldn't conquer, it's probably because the enemy has set up camp in a corner of your mind. This is also known as a stronghold, and you can only remove it with God's help. We'll talk more about that in a minute.

FIGHTING OTHERS

Many of my destructive thought patterns have been influenced by the negative expressions of others. For years, I allowed their destructive actions and words to infiltrate my thinking.

Remember the job I left? One person I worked with was condescending. This person's actions and words planted seeds of doubt, anger, criticism, and self-condemnation in my thought life. Too often, those thoughts overtook my mind like weeds and I began to feel discouraged, which had a negative impact on my work. Other people will be happy to influence your thoughts for the worse to gain power over you.

You may also have people in your life who are naysayers. Others may tell you things in a conscious or subconscious attempt to hold you down. I understand what abuse feels like, and the messages, whether silent or spoken, are strong. They creep their way into your thought life, sabotaging your attempts to live the life God wants for you.

If others are working against your thought-life transformation, you'll find good news in the next section. God will provide the help you need.

MEDITATING ON GOD'S WORD

Romans 8:6 states, "The mind governed by the flesh is death, but the mind governed by the Spirit is life and peace." Let's begin our first meditation exercise with this verse.

The mind governed

You are always handing power over to either the good or bad side with your thoughts. Take a moment and read Job 1:6–12. From this account, we can see that our lives are battlegrounds in the spiritual realm. Your good, healthy thoughts are pleasing to God, and your negative, destructive thoughts are pleasing to the enemy.

by the flesh

Our flesh is our sinful human nature. My sinful human nature always moves toward what is easy, painless, and lazy. The center of fleshly thoughts is selfishness. Most of my unchecked thoughts follow that self-centered path. But I don't want my thoughts to be governed by my flesh, which is weak and flabby. I'm sure you are longing for transformation just like I am.

is death

This phrase is like a mirror in natural light that shows the naked truth. If I allow my flesh-based thoughts to rule my life, I am no different from the rest of the world. I would be miserable and stuck, headed down a slippery path of destruction. If I didn't give my thoughts and my whole life over to God for healthy transformation, I would be condemned to eternal death.

but the mind governed by the Spirit

God is so gracious to provide us a choice. Like a good parent, he sets rules for us to follow because he loves us, wants the best for us, and wants to protect us from harm. We can choose a different path. We can submit our thoughts to the Holy Spirit's rule and enjoy God's blessings.

is life and peace.

Isn't this what we all want—peace in our days? According to Jesus, nothing will be able to remove every trouble while we are here on earth (John 16:33). But life and peace are possible, even abundant, through the Holy Spirit's governance. We can destroy the enemy's strongholds, win the flesh-based war, and avoid death by submitting our thoughts to the Holy Spirit.

Congratulations on completing your first meditation exercise! Now let's look at how the Holy Spirit will help you fight the battles ahead.

HOPE IN THE SPIRIT

The Holy Spirit is the main agent in your thought-life transformation. His roles are perfectly suited for sweeping your mind clear of junk drawer clutter and filling it with ordered truth.

When I began my thought-life transformation years ago, I prayed that the Holy Spirit would prick my conscience whenever I had a wayward thought that would lead to trouble. That prayer received a resounding yes as an answer. Let's just say that my brain got "pinged" several hundred times a day when I first started out. With practice, I've come to recognize the Holy Spirit's working in my life, and my mind is more settled than it's ever been due to his working.

One of the Holy Spirit's main roles is to enlighten our minds. He is the Spirit of truth who guides us into all truth (John 16:13). By meditating on God's Word, you firmly place his truth inside your mind. It will refute the lies you encounter in the fight against yourself, your enemy, and others. Day by day, God's Word will tear down the enemy's strongholds.

Jesus said that the Holy Spirit teaches us and reminds us of his words. As you begin regular Christian meditation, the Holy Spirit will teach you about the Bible and bring God's Word to mind at the perfect time. This has happened countless times to me, whether I'm speaking with my children or writing a blog post. I'm always amazed at the Holy Spirit's ability to bring an ideal verse of Scripture to mind right when I need it, after I've done the work of hiding it inside.

Another wonderful role of the Holy Spirit is interceding for you (Rom. 8:27). He is praying on your behalf, asking God the Father to renew your mind. Does this bring you joy like it does for me? It means I'm not alone in this journey. . . . I have a member of the triune God working for my benefit! How's that for a power boost?

If you have struggled in your thought life for a long time, take hope that the Holy Spirit is your mediator, advocate, and counselor. He will equip you and defend your cause before the enemy. He will guide you into fruitful, purpose-filled thinking, rather than fruitless, careless thinking. You are never alone in this battle.

THE DISCIPLINE OF MEDITATION

Think about an area in which you are an "expert." It doesn't mean you have your own TV show on the topic, conduct lectures on it, or even make a dime doing it. What is something you're good at?

One thing I've gotten good at is gardening. I've kept my own garden since I was thirteen years old. I read many library books to learn about gardening. Real-life lessons from pests, diseases, drought, and floods taught me well. For years, I attended seminars conducted by master gardeners and I quizzed them about my garden problems. I've planted thousands of plants in hundreds of varieties over the years, and I tend my own indoor jungle too. The only way I improved my gardening skills was through practice.

Practice was essential for me learning how to play the flute, speak French, bake sweets, and paint with acrylics. I give God all the credit for giving me creative talents. But I didn't excel in any of these pursuits without many hours of practice.

Taking control of your thought life also takes practice. It may not feel natural or comfortable at first. It may feel painful to let go of deeply entrenched patterns of thought. But with the help of the Holy Spirit, your thought life will be transformed by God's life and peace.

When do your thoughts wander the most? Is it during drives, chores, meetings, or (ahem) sermons? Know your triggers, and quickly meditate on a verse to get back on track in those moments.

My mind wanders most in the late afternoon. I think it's because I'm tired from a day of work, yet I know there's more work to be finished in the evening (a mom's work is never done). I tend to let my mind "play" around 4:00 P.M., and before I know it, my mind has strayed into prohibited territory.

The theme verse for this chapter is an excellent meditation prompt any time your thoughts get careless. Let's look at 2 Corinthians 10:5 closely.

We take captive every thought

Remember catching fireflies as a child? When the firefly was inside the jar, you could see it up close. Its light wasn't a spark in the distance anymore. You could see its wings open and close, and notice the light blinked from the end of its abdomen. You could count its six legs if you liked. The firefly was under your inspection.

Taking your thoughts captive is like catching fireflies. You need to hold the thoughts closely for a moment, examining them for what they are. Not making excuses for them, but simply studying them.

to make it obedient to Christ.

When you examine your thoughts, you need to ask yourself, "Is this thought obedient to Christ?" Another way of processing it is to ask yourself, "Would I feel good about sharing this thought aloud with Jesus?" If your thought doesn't pass through the obedience filter, you can quickly confess it and repent, replacing your thought with an obedient one.

I'll give you an example. If my mind wanders during a sermon, I catch my careless thought in a mental jar and silently pray, "I'm sorry, Lord, for not listening. Thank you for placing me here in this church. Help me focus on the message you want me to hear today." My slate is clean, and I'm ready to listen again.

The discipline of meditation is not intended to be a guilt machine. It's simply capturing and filtering thoughts to have a mind more like Jesus. He knows that we can't possibly process every thought that travels through our minds. Yet the more discipline we apply, the more thoughts will go through the obedience filter and the more obedient we will become.

PURSUING INTENTION

In each chapter, we'll reflect on a different virtue that can help us grow in meditation. To begin, let's consider the value of pursuing God with intention with our thoughts. Instead of letting our minds roam freely, our spiritual growth can flourish if we learn the value of intention. James tells us that we should look intently into God's perfect law (James 1:25). When you take that intentional look into his Word, you gain freedom and blessing as you put his principles into action. Meditation helps you retain Scripture so you don't forget it. When you retain it, you can apply it much more effectively.

Proverbs explains that God's instruction is beyond comparison and more important than silver, gold, and rubies (Prov. 8:10–11). Intentional living is about making wise and thoughtful choices. Through meditation we can choose God's instruction, knowledge, and wisdom, which are worth far more than the world's finest offerings. Intentionally focusing on Scripture through meditation will help you choose God's best for your life by taking each thought captive for examination and correction.

MORE MEDITATION VERSES

ↄ For you look deep within the mind and heart, O righteous God. (Ps. 7:9b NLT)

ↄ Test me, LORD, and try me; examine my heart and my mind. (Ps. 26:2)

ↄ Jesus replied: "You must love the Lord your God with all your heart, all your soul, and all your mind." (Matt. 22:37 NLT)

ↄ Do not conform to the pattern of this world, but be transformed by the renewing of your mind. Then you will be able to test and approve what God's will is—his good, pleasing and perfect will. (Rom. 12:2)

ↄ But you should keep a clear mind in every situation. (2 Tim. 4:5b NLT)

ↄ "This is the new covenant I will make with my people on that day," says the LORD: "I will put my laws in their hearts, and I will write them on their minds." (Heb. 10:16 NLT)

Prayer

Father in heaven,

I praise you because you created a world of order. Your design is masterful. You designed my mind to be ordered as well.

I confess that I often allow my thoughts to carelessly stray into places where they don't belong. The roots of many of my problems lie in these wayward places. I admit that sometimes I go there of my own will, and I want to make changes today.

Thank you for offering me life and peace through a renewed mind. Thank you that I have the Holy Spirit as my guide, helper, and teacher. You have promised to never leave me nor forsake me, and I trust that you won't leave me alone in my thought-life transformation.

Prick my conscience when my thoughts are careless, Lord. Help me capture them and see them for what they are without getting defensive. Help me meditate upon your Word so I have it ready to go when temptation strikes.

I lift this prayer up in the name of Jesus,
Amen.

REFLECTION QUESTIONS

1. What is the connection between your current problems and your thought life?

2. What is your biggest area of struggle: fighting yourself, fighting the enemy, or fighting others? Why?

3. What comforts you most about the Holy Spirit's role in transforming your thought life?

NOTE

[1]Bill and Pam Farrel, *Men Are Like Waffles, Women Are Like Spaghetti* (Eugene, OR: Harvest House, 2001), 13.

CHAPTER TWO

NEGATIVE THOUGHTS

The precepts of the Lord are right,
giving joy to the heart. The commands of the
Lord are radiant, giving life to the eyes.

—PSALM 19:8

Have you ever taken a personality test? I am somewhat addicted to them. I'm an INFJ on the Myers-Briggs scale and an Enneagram 1. The common thread between all the tests I've taken is my melancholy perspective.

God made me a supersensitive person with a passion for high quality. This means I'm more likely than others to notice and feel the hard things in life. Lows are naturally lower for me, and a positive perspective is a challenge. My glass is almost always half-empty.

The way I grew up reinforced my natural negative bent. As a child of divorce at the age of four, my world was permanently affected by a living death. I became responsible overnight since my stay-at-home mom had to find work. I also have a photographic memory, and I keenly remember fumbling with the buttons on my plaid shirt while I got myself ready for kindergarten one morning. I couldn't ask anyone for help. A negative thought ran through my mind: "This isn't the way things should be." But I was powerless to change my situation.

I didn't realize this until I was an adult, but my family had a negative communication style. Instead of getting counseling for our various issues, our family conversations revolved around past and current drama. I believe we were trying to process our pain the best we could, but we weren't equipped to do it ourselves. The same stories played over and over for decades, like records that were never switched out. Their grooves were deeply worn.

My divorced parents didn't really want to hear about each other when we visited their homes. I felt frustrated because I had to edit my stories and hide details to save their feelings. My sister and I would lie in our shared bedroom in either home and vent our frustrations, spilling out our pent-up negative thoughts to each other. Even though we were only children, we were forming our own negative patterns and reinforcing them every time we changed locations.

Negative thoughts ruled my world as a teenager, as they do for so many teens. I kept most of them inside, letting them out only to my best friend. When she moved away the autumn of our junior year, my thoughts became so dark that I fell into a suicidal depression. I felt a heavy weight on my body from my dark thoughts, like the vest the dental assistant puts on you before you get X-rays. It held me downward, and more negative thoughts rained on me every day from a dark cloud the sun couldn't break through.

God rescued me from the pit of my depression before I took action on my self-destructive plans. One afternoon when I was lying in bed, contemplating methods, I suddenly felt the presence of God in the room, warm and comforting. The Holy Spirit whispered this message to me: "You don't need to think these thoughts anymore." I got up and never considered suicide again. I grew up in the church with a healthy fear of God, and it helped me stay out of that pit. I didn't want to risk making God upset with my disobedient thoughts.

Looking back at that moment now, I see that God cared deeply about my thought life. He knew that my negative thoughts were literally leading me on a path toward death, and he wanted me to choose the path of life. That late autumn afternoon in 1993 was a turning point in my thought life. I knew my thoughts counted for something, and I knew they had to change.

In the years that followed, I still had many negative circumstances and relationships to sort out. But starting at age sixteen, I began choosing positive thoughts, even though my natural bend falls toward negative thoughts.

One way I balance my melancholy perspective is by surrounding myself with optimists. One of my dear friends always has sunshine to share, and I value her uplifting perspective. However, I know she sometimes struggles with negative feelings, related to deep hurts. Even the sunniest personality experiences the rain of negativity.

Whether you have a naturally optimistic or melancholy personality, I'm certain that you engage in a fight with negative thoughts every single day. Through the power of the Holy Spirit, we can learn to focus on joy instead of negativity.

THE POWER OF JOYFUL THOUGHTS

Joy is like a new friend I admire. She smiles often and seems at peace, even on a bad hair day. Her clothes are pretty and colorful, though she doesn't wear the trendiest styles. She laughs a lot more often than I do. Joy always wears sparkles, whether on her earrings or fingernails, because they make life brighter. She's gone through similar trials, but her outlook is so different. So much better. She is always content, even when life tempts her to sulk or cry.

I want to get to know her better, but I keep forgetting to call. Do you need to invite Joy into your life too? I think we'll both feel better after a visit with her.

Joy is contentment within our circumstances. In 2 Corinthians, the apostle Paul lists many hardships he and his team endured for the sake of ministry. Within his painful list, he speaks of joy: "Our hearts ache, but we always have joy. We are poor, but we give our spiritual riches to others. We own nothing, and yet we have everything" (2 Cor. 6:10 NLT).

The source of Paul's joy is the same for us: worshipping and serving the one true God.

Having joy doesn't mean we pretend our lives are free from problems. Joy helps us find peace in the middle of pain, because God is good no matter what. Joy looks forward to a brighter future when no suffering, tears, or negativity will exist. Hope is another close companion of Joy. We can focus on joy when we hope in the treasures God has waiting for us.

When you have a heavenly mind-set rather than an earthly mind-set, joyful thoughts are easier to find. Recently I began a study on the book of Ephesians. The first chapter of Ephesians is a treasure chest full of God's blessings that we can enjoy both now and in the future.

Let's meditate on some of these blessings from the New Living Translation. Read over them slowly, savoring the riches:

> *All praise to God, the Father of our Lord Jesus Christ, who has blessed us with every spiritual blessing in the heavenly realms because we are united with Christ. (Eph. 1:3)*

We have every spiritual blessing awaiting us in heaven, because we are one with Christ. This verse alone can kill negative thoughts on the spot. You can meditate on this verse to feel joyful, and add others from this chapter to feel even more joy.

Even before he made the world, God loved us and chose us in Christ to be holy and without fault in his eyes. (Eph. 1:4)

Long before you were born, God chose you to be his daughter. He sees you as flawless because Jesus died for you. Isn't it wonderful to consider that he claimed you as his own before you realized it? Bask in the glow of this verse, and let joy fill your heart.

God decided in advance to adopt us into his own family by bringing us to himself through Jesus Christ. This is what he wanted to do, and it gave him great pleasure. (Eph. 1:5)

God delights in adopting you into his family. Can you imagine your sinless, perfect Father taking pleasure in calling you his princess? Because God gets joy from bringing us closer to him, we can also take joy in knowing that he wants us to feel a sense of belonging in his kingdom.

The Spirit is God's guarantee that he will give us the inheritance he promised and that he has purchased us to be his own people. He did this so we would praise and glorify him. (Eph. 1:14)

The presence of the Holy Spirit in your heart is proof that you belong to God. The inheritance of heaven is guaranteed by the Holy Spirit's presence. As he helps you overcome your thought-life problems, praise him for serving as a reminder of your heavenly inheritance.

My thoughts feel uplifted simply from thinking about those verses. They hold great power to inspire joy in our hearts. Joy is lighter than negativity. It rises to the top like a life preserver that rescues us from our negative thoughts. Next time you feel the waves of negativity threatening to pull you under, choose a verse of Scripture that points you to God's blessings. Take joy in God's promises and use it to lift you up over negative thoughts.

MEDITATE ON GOD'S WORD

It's important to note that the source of our joy must come from God. Our world is full of pain, and it will drag us down if we allow it. Tracie Miles writes, "Any negative thought that goes uncaptured will eventually cause us to sink."[1]

Job was a man well acquainted with pain. In a single day, he lost many of his most precious treasures—his animals, which were his livelihood, and all his beloved children. Then, because he didn't curse God after the tragic losses, the enemy struck him with painful sores from head to toe. Job complained in righteous lament, but still hung on to his faith.

In all his pain, Job attributed his source of joy to God's Word. He found consolation in not denying the words of the Holy God (Job 6:10). I think it's safe to say that Job still holds the Olympic record for suffering. If he found joy in God's Word despite his situation, we can too.

When David wrote Psalm 19, he also turned to God's Word as a source of joy. He wrote that the precepts and commands of the Lord are right and radiant (Ps. 19:8). God's Word is the ultimate source of joy and life, and by practicing Christian meditation, you'll have a constant source of joy in your mind to counter those negative thoughts.

Many of you readers are mothers. Without exception, every mother I've known has experienced pain before, during, and after childbirth. But the first time you hear your baby's cry and hold him or her in your arms, the most powerful anesthetic in the world takes away your pain: joy!

I love that Jesus used childbirth as an illustration for joy. In John 16:21–22, he compares our daily suffering and grief to the pain of childbirth. When we meet with Jesus each day, his presence in our hearts brings fresh joy that no one can take away from us.

He spoke these words to his disciples the night before he died. He promised that their joy would last on and on after they experienced his resurrection. You and I can always rejoice in the fulfillment of that promise, even if our current painful situation is as intense as childbirth. Joy is always waiting for us on the opposite side of our negativity.

JOY-BOOSTING THOUGHT EXERCISES

No other book in the Bible lists joy more often than Psalms. Meditating on the Psalms will give you many ways to replace negative thoughts with joyful ones.

You have an assignment as a Christian: be joyful! Psalm 68:3 charges us to put on a joyful, glad, and happy attitude. It's so tempting to be a sour-faced Christian with all of life's troubles—I'm guilty of that failure far too often. Joy is our witnessing tool to the world, and we need to remember to show it.

Start your morning seeking joy from God's Word, and the rest of your day will be better. Psalm 90:14 tells us to seek God's love in the morning so we can find joy. This has proven true in my life. For the past seventeen years, I've started my day with God's Word, and it always sets a positive tone for my day.

Nature is always praising God with joy. Psalm 65:8 tells us that the Lord calls songs of joy forth from the earth's wonders, and they are especially apparent at sunrise and sunset. Take a walk today or look outside your window, at sunrise or sunset if possible, and praise God for the joy that is so visible in his creation.

Remember that the mind controlled by the Spirit has life and peace? In Psalm 16:11, we learn that God's Word shows us the path to life, which gives us joy and reveals eternal pleasures to us. When you are searching out the path for your life, God promises to give you joy and pleasure if you walk with him at your side.

When you feel weak, you can rely on God's strength and protection as you trust him. Psalm 28:7 says he is your strength and shield. Your trust in his protection will stir up joy in your heart. You may even want to break out in songs of praise, as the verse suggests.

If you sing, use your voice to praise God with joy. Psalm 43:4 urges us to make music to praise God as our source of joy. If you play an instrument, perform a private concert of praise for your Lord. Even if you can't sing, you can listen to praise music and practice joy as the song plays.

David wrote Psalm 51 when he repented of his sins. In verse 12, he asked God to restore the joy of his salvation. After confession, you can take joy in the fact that God forgives you and makes you totally clean. You can also rejoice that God generously upholds you with the Holy Spirit, because you are precious to him.

Even in times of grief, we can have joy because those painful times don't last forever. Psalm 30:11 shows us that God will turn our mourning into dancing. God has the power to clothe us with joy from head to foot. He inspires us to dance with joy, wearing our new clothes of celebration.

An easy way to find joy is to recount God's blessings to you. When we recount all the things he has done for us, we will be filled with joy (Ps. 126:3). Remembering his faithfulness will inspire new praise, which will wipe out negative thoughts.

Anytime you need fresh inspiration for countering your negative thoughts, simply enter "joy" in the search box on biblegateway.

com and go to the book of Psalms. Pick the translation you like best and use God's Word as your source for busting negativity.

MORE MEDITATION VERSES

- ✌ He will yet fill your mouth with laughter and your lips with shouts of joy. (Job 8:21)

- ✌ You will go out in joy and be led forth in peace. (Isa. 55:12)

- ✌ But the angel said to them, "Do not be afraid. I bring you good news that will cause great joy for all the people." (Luke 2:10)

- ✌ You haven't done this before. Ask, using my name, and you will receive, and you will have abundant joy. (John 16:24 NLT)

- ✌ May the God of hope fill you with all joy and peace as you trust in him, so that you may overflow with hope by the power of the Holy Spirit. (Rom. 15:13)

- ✌ Though you have not seen him, you love him. Though you do not now see him, you believe in him and rejoice with joy that is inexpressible and filled with glory. (1 Pet. 1:8 ESV)

Father in heaven,

You are worthy of praise because you have chosen such greatness for me. How wonderful it is that you share your riches with me! I am brought to my knees in humility.

I often forget that you are my source of joy, because I let my problems weigh me down. I know that life will always be a challenge, but I want to choose your ways over mine from now on. I choose joy instead of negativity.

Thank you for providing abundant verses on joy in your Word, Lord. Help me select ones that will lift me up when I'm drowning in negativity. I trust that you will guide me into the truth of your Word, which will transform my thinking. Thank you for renewing my mind.

In Jesus's name,
Amen.

REFLECTION QUESTIONS

1. How did your childhood impact your struggle with negative thoughts?

2. Which verse in Ephesians 1 means the most to you, and why?

3. Do you have a favorite verse from the book of Psalms? How can you use it to transform your negative thoughts?

NOTE

[1]Tracie Miles, *Unsinkable Faith: God-Filled Strategies to Transform the Way You Think, Feel, and Live* (Colorado Springs: David C. Cook, 2017), 161.

CHAPTER THREE

ANXIOUS THOUGHTS

Search me, O God, and know my heart;
test me and know my anxious thoughts.

—PSALM 139:23

Recently I was scrolling through my Facebook feed, and in a few short clicks, I found myself in anxiety's grip. A notification from a childhood friend led me to photos from our twentieth high school reunion a few years ago. Perhaps since I chose not to attend any of the reunions, the pictures intrigued me.

As I sifted through pictures of smiling thirty-eight-year-old faces, anxiety tightened my stomach and moved up my esophagus and into my throat, making it harder to breathe. My heartbeat galloped as I looked at those faces, and I couldn't believe the power of the pixels to trap me in anxiety within moments.

I took several deep breaths and asked myself why I was feeling so anxious. The answer became clear: My high school years were the worst ones of my life. Even though I've faced many challenging seasons, nothing compares to the unhappiness, stress, and negativity I experienced then.

As a freshman, I transferred from a small private school class of twenty-four that felt like family to a large class of almost three hundred strangers in public school. Had I been more extroverted or gotten to know peers through sports, this shift might not have been so difficult. But I never got over feeling like an outsider. The big crowds felt threatening, especially when I endured being bullied in my freshman and sophomore years.

I excelled in academics, befriending more teachers than classmates. As noted in the previous chapter, my best friend moved away at the beginning of junior year. Her leaving coincided with unprocessed family problems, which landed me in a suicidal depression. A few failed dating relationships only increased my feelings of social awkwardness in this tumultuous time.

During my senior year, my drama class elected me as a candidate for fall homecoming queen. I couldn't believe they would choose an unsocial, overweight, quiet girl like me. With reluctance, I attended the event. My escort joked with me as we walked down the center of the football field, where I pasted on a smile for the yearbook photographer. I posed with the other candidates before the crowning, and I danced the requisite dance. When that first song was over, I told my escort I needed a bathroom break. But I left as fast as I could, thankful for the darkness of night that hid my escape.

Leaving that dance gave me the confidence to keep leaving. For the rest of my senior year, I drove home to eat lunch by myself. When the end-of-year senior activities arrived, I refused to attend almost every one, including prom. I told my mom not to throw me a graduation party, because I didn't want to celebrate those four years in any way.

On the first day of college, I inhaled deeply and exhaled a sigh of relief in the hot, humid August morning, even though I was surrounded by a huge crowd of students as I walked to class. I faced no more social pressure from those three hundred high school classmates. No more scrutiny over who I was dating, what I was wearing, or who I befriended. No more reminders of my failures with peers. The anonymity of the university campus held strong appeal. I thought it would squash my social anxiety forever.

The truth is, I still struggle with some social anxiety. Working as a secretary in a high school for four years didn't help. My best friend quipped that the irony wasn't lost on her; I was doing time in the jail of my adolescence. Every time homecoming, prom, or graduation rolled around, I shrank back or fled like I did when I was seventeen.

As a staff member, I was required to attend graduation. I donned the cap and gown and played my role, pasting on a smile again. But every time, I tucked my keys in my waistband so I could leave immediately, without having to deal with the social pressure of saying goodbye or congratulations to hundreds of people.

My maiden surname means "to take flight" in German. Maybe it's coded into my DNA. Not literally, mind you; flying in an airplane produces a different kind of anxiety for me. Yet I'm a pro at taking flight from social pressure, because the anxiety that seizes my gut pushes me up and away.

YOUR KIND OF ANXIETY

Maybe social anxiety is your struggle, or maybe it isn't. But I'm sure that you struggle with some form of anxiety, because many women in our fast-paced culture do.[1]

I know women who are anxious about their children, wondering whether they are messing them up with "bad" parenting. In fact, I don't know a mom who hasn't worried about her children's safety or choices, no matter how young or old her children are.

One woman I know has had decades-long anxiety over health. Since she unexpectedly lost her baby, she hasn't stopped worrying that any other loved one could suddenly die from unexpected illness. Her exaggerated concern over coughs and fevers is simply a manifestation of her deepest fear—losing a loved one to poor health again.

I know women who struggle with anxiety over their weight, wrinkles, and hair loss (or hair growth in unwanted areas). Their anxiety is rooted in fear of losing their beauty. We'll talk about this more in Chapter Four.

We women worry about our marriages, careers, finances, and futures. We worry about politics and what to cook for dinner. We worry about terrorism while we worry about how to save for retirement. Let's face it; we women are expert worriers. Our worst worries are often connected to our oldest, deepest fears.

This chapter is not meant to address anxiety disorders that require medication to control. It's meant to address the roots of anxiety common to most of us women, who allow anxiety to take over our minds without even realizing it.

What are your anxiety triggers? Let's meditate on Psalm 139:23 to discover them, so we can deal with them.

Search me, O God, and know my heart

Do you realize that God knows everything that goes on in your heart and mind? He is like a highway patrolman who never needs sleep. His radar catches all kinds of anxious thoughts that speed through your mind, day or night. He's already got tabs on what fears reside in your heart that prompt anxiety, and he wants to help you identify those thoughts, so you can make progress.

test me and know my anxious thoughts.

When you ask God to search you, know you, and test you, he will most certainly answer that prayer. The Holy Spirit will begin to show you exactly which anxious thoughts you have and where they reside. He'll start pointing them out when they zip through your mind, trying to speed by without being noticed. He will help you catch them, prosecute them, and remove their power over you.

WHEN ANXIETY THREATENS

Take a moment to think about the physical sensations you feel when you are anxious. I know I'm anxious when my insides tighten, my breath shortens, and my heart starts racing. Sometimes it feels like I'm being strangled when anxiety takes hold.

The original meaning of the word *worry* means "to strangle or choke." Author Linda Dillow says, "The stranglehold of worry keeps a woman from enjoying a life of contentment and peace."[2]

What happens to your body when worry takes over? Knowing this can help you identify anxiety and deal with it right away.

Recently, my husband lost his wallet. All morning, I prayed off and on that he would find it. I ordered lunch from the Panera drive-through. As I sat in line, I noticed my insides tightening. My thoughts had gone down a wild path in only seconds; suddenly, I was picturing a criminal wiping out our bank accounts with stolen cards. Anxiety had a foothold and was gaining ground with every heartbeat.

Then the Holy Spirit spoke to me: *What verse can you meditate on right now?* I took a moment to capture my thoughts, then remembered the verse displayed on a card in my kitchen windowsill: "Call upon me in the day of trouble: I will deliver you, and you shall glorify me" (Psalm 50:15 ESV).

On my dashboard, I tapped the verse into a rhythm, repeating it again and again, then turned it into a prayer. I remembered many other people in the Bible who faced greater problems than mine, and how God delivered them. I promised to glorify God and give him all the credit if the wallet was found. Calm washed over me after I prayed.

Later that day, my husband told me he found the wallet on his own job site. It had fallen out of his new shorts pocket, which wasn't as deep as the others. The wallet was never in the hands of a stranger. It was always in God's care, and I gave him the praise for growing my faith with that little test.

DEALING WITH ANXIETY THROUGH MEDITATION

The Bible offers a rich variety of verses to help us deal with anxiety. You can use these verses as shields and arrows in your battles.

Does anxiety or worry feel heavy to you? They definitely weigh me down, as described in Proverbs 12:25. This verse tells us that an encouraging word from a friend or loved one lifts me up. But if I'm alone, I can still be uplifted with a positive verse of the Bible about God's character. This verse keeps me in check, because if I want my heart to feel lighter, I must offload anxious thoughts.

Who among us doesn't have a secret multitude of anxieties? I love Psalm 94:19 because it tells me that God knows my heart. He offers comfort to offset the weight of anxieties. The Latin root for comfort is the same one we use for "fortress," a symbol of strength. God's comfort isn't soft or flimsy. It's meant to strengthen us in our battles. God's supernatural strength delights us, because we know we don't face our battles in our own power.

The short, sweet verse of 1 Peter 5:7 reminds us that God is strong enough to handle all our anxieties. They aren't too heavy for him, though they are surely too heavy for us. He wants us to cast our anxieties on him, like casting a fishing line out on a pond, throwing them far away from us and onto him. This verse tells us God is willing to handle our anxieties because he deeply loves us.

PURSUING PEACE

To truly conquer anxiety, we must focus our thoughts on peace when we feel anxious. As a young woman, anxiety ruled my life. But when I participated in a Bible study in 2005 on the book *Calm My Anxious Heart* by Linda Dillow, God set me free from the paralyzing grip anxiety had on my heart.

In her book, Dillow refers to God again and again as the blessed controller of all things, as found in 1 Timothy 6:15.[3] Her book helped me see that my struggle with anxiety was rooted in my desire to pursue control, and that control only belongs to God, who is sovereign over every detail of my life. He showed me that when I cast my anxiety on him by handing it over to him in my mind, he allowed his peace to enter into the places where anxiety once took up space. I truly don't struggle with it every day anymore, since his perfect peace is firmly fixed in my heart.

Jesus's peace isn't neutral; it's miraculous peace that carries us through the most difficult circumstances. In John 14:27, Jesus promises to give us peace that is different from the temporary, circumstance-based peace the world offers. His perfect peace will drive fear from our hearts and still our troubles into calm trust.

Jesus spoke this verse to his disciples on the night he was betrayed. The night all the disciples would desert him with anxiety filling their hearts to the breaking point. The day before he would be stripped, beaten, and crucified. In those terribly imminent circumstances, Jesus offered his peace. He told them not to let their hearts be troubled, because he knew they would be tempted to fear for their lives. He offered them perfect peace in the middle of the worst anxiety they had ever faced.

Jesus offers the same peace to me and you. The Bible tells us to "seek peace and pursue it" in Psalm 34:14. We must actively search for it when anxiety rises. We must fix verses in our minds and hearts to be ready when the battle ensues.

Philippians 4:6–7 offers a detailed action plan for pursuing peace when anxiety strikes.

1. Pray about everything that causes worry. Don't leave anything out. Whether it's a wasp in your house or a loved one's open-heart surgery, every anxiety-producing trigger is a call to pray for help from the blessed controller over all creation.
2. Tell God exactly what you need. If you need him to help you find a wallet, kill a spider, or have strength while you wait, make a specific request of him. When we list our requests to Almighty God, anxiety loses its power.
3. Thank him for all he has done. Remembering God's faithfulness to you when you feel anxious will ground you in his unchanging character. Recounting times when he pulled you through in the past will help you believe that he can pull you through again.
4. Enjoy the flood of peace that rushes over your heart. After you release your anxiety through requests and thanksgiving, God's peace will set a guard over your heart and mind. His peace will set you free to live in obedience, even if your worrisome circumstance hasn't changed.

Don't you love the practical application of these two verses? Put them into action when anxiety threatens, and your peace will be restored.

In 2017, I chose Isaiah 26:3 as my theme verse of the year. I created a graphic and made it the screensaver of my desktop computer.

Every morning, I saw this verse before I started writing. It carried me through a tough transition, because it reminded me to keep my mind steadfast on God's promises rather than my worries, so I could experience his peace despite the unknown outcome. My trust in him grew as I meditated on this powerful verse hundreds of times. It will work powerful change in your life as well.

Sue Detweiler writes, "To replace your anxiety with his unshakable peace requires that you trust him. Choose to take heart and focus on the fact that Jesus overcame, so you can too. He is the God of peace who crushes anxiety under your feet [as described in Romans 16:20 ESV]."[4] I love the picture of Jesus crushing anxiety, just as he was destined to crush the enemy's head in Genesis 3:15.

MORE MEDITATION VERSES

- A heart at peace gives life to the body. (Prov. 14:30)

- LORD, you establish peace for us; all that we have accomplished you have done for us. (Isa. 26:12)

- And this righteousness will bring peace. Yes, it will bring quietness and confidence forever. (Isa. 32:17 NLT)

- "May they have peace, both near and far, for I will heal them all," says the LORD. (Isa. 57:19 NLT)

- "Glory to God in the highest heaven, and peace on earth to all whom God favors." (Luke 2:14 NLT)

- Therefore, since we have been made right in God's sight by faith, we have peace with God because of what Jesus Christ our Lord has done for us. (Rom. 5:1 NLT)

- Stand firm then . . . with your feet fitted with the readiness that comes from the gospel of peace. (Eph. 6:14–15)

- Let the peace of Christ rule in your hearts, since as members of one body you were called to peace. (Col. 3:15)

- Now may the Lord of peace himself give you peace at all times in every way. The Lord be with you all. (2 Thess. 3:16 ESV)

Prayer

Father in heaven,

I praise you because you are the blessed controller over every detail of my life. You know my heart and my mind better than anyone else, and you claim them for your glory.

I confess that I often let anxiety control my thoughts. I admit that my anxiety is often connected to a desire to control my circumstances, but I declare today that only you have control over my life.

Thank you for being faithful to me in all my past times of anxiety. Thank you for never leaving me alone in my worries. You have delivered me time and time again, and I trust that you will help me replace anxiety with your perfect peace.

Send your Holy Spirit to reveal my anxiety triggers. Show me the multitude of my anxieties and help me conquer each one through the power of your Word.

In Jesus's name,
Amen.

REFLECTION QUESTIONS

1. What are the physical symptoms of anxiety for you?

2. When do you feel anxiety is worst for you? What times of day, month, and year? These are the best times to meditate on God's Word.

3. Which verse gave you the most peace? How can you use it to fight off anxiety?

NOTES

[1] Jacqueline Howard, "Why Women Are Way More Likely Than Men to Suffer Anxiety," CNN, June 8, 2016, https://www.cnn.com/2016/06/08/health/women-anxiety-disorders/index.html.

[2] Linda Dillow, *Calm My Anxious Heart: A Woman's Guide to Finding Contentment* (Colorado Springs: Navpress, 1998), 120.

[3] Dillow, *Calm My Anxious Heart,* 41.

[4] Sue Detweiler, *Women Who Move Mountains: Praying with Confidence, Boldness, and Grace* (Minneapolis: Bethany House, 2017), 96.

CHAPTER FOUR

SELF-CRITICAL THOUGHTS

I praise you because I am fearfully and
wonderfully made; your works are wonderful,
I know that full well.

—PSALM 139:14

In the summer between third and fourth grade, before I turned nine years old, my body started changing from a little girl into a young woman. That's when my DNA started sending messages to my lower stomach, under my navel, to form what I named my hump. I guess it reminded me of a camel's hump when I was young, except it is on my stomach rather than my back.

My DNA was programmed with threads of lengthy directions from one side of my family, where the hump had formed on women's bodies for generations. Yet my hump was so strange to me that I couldn't resist attacking it with self-criticism. I tried to negate it with vicious, attacking words in my head. The battle of self-criticism began then and has raged for decades.

My hump has made me look two or three months pregnant ever since I was a child. I quickly learned that hiding my hump was a major priority, because other children didn't hide their criticism of it. I thank God I became a teen in the 1990s, when big, baggy clothes were in. I could wear my dad's extra-large flannel shirts and still receive compliments, without anyone noticing my hump. Cheers for the long, blousy tops that are in style now too!

My weight has fluctuated through the years, like it has for many of you. No matter how thin I got, my hump was always there. The only time it "disappeared" was when I was pregnant. The more I weigh, the bigger it is, but it does shrink if I lose weight. It's a sort of biological indicator of when I need to eat less and exercise more.

Many times, I've reasoned that I'd look just fine if my hump was gone. I wouldn't look perfect, but I wouldn't look or feel so odd. Of course, that's the moment I study myself in the mirror and find quite a few other things I'd like to change. My mind moves downward in a self-critical spiral.

This battle over my body image has lasted for decades, and I'm ready for it to stop.

I've seen commercials for injections and cold laser treatments that promise to remove stubborn fat cells. Some advertisements even say something like, "I know I have my mom's double chin, but I want to make it my own." I'm choosing to accept that my hump is permanently programmed to be in my body. Even if I tried to physically remove my hump, I know it would come right back, because the mysterious power of DNA is stronger than a knife, needle, or laser.

A few years ago, I was drying off after my shower and caught a full-length glimpse of myself in the mirror. Before turning away in my normal disgust, God whisper-shouted to me, *"You are fearfully and wonderfully made—LOOK!"* He led me to look at myself—my whole body—and call it good. Even my hump. When I called my hump "good" for the first time, I felt a new peace come over me. I opened my heart to loving my body just the way it is, without wishing for change.

The hard truth is that God knew ahead of time that I would have a hump because he programmed my DNA cells. This wasn't easy to accept at first, because it doesn't make sense to me. But the more I learned about God, the more I realized I cannot call anything that he made "bad." He knew what he was doing, and even though I don't understand it, he understands me perfectly as my master designer.

I'm sure that you have a particular body part, inherited trait, or quirky characteristic that you cannot stand, and you probably don't know what God was thinking when he gave it to you. Maybe you can't stand the mind you've been given, or the gifts or talents he's given you. Maybe you don't like the way you sound when you talk or laugh. Maybe you simply don't like yourself, period.

I am well acquainted with that self-destructive internal dialogue many of us experience but none of us freely talk about. You aren't alone in this battle. God cares about you and wants to transform your self-criticism with his love. He wants to help you love yourself, which you must do before you can love others well.

TESTING FOR SELF-CRITICISM

How often do words like these go through your mind unchecked?

- Stupid
- Worthless
- Bad
- Dumb
- Ignorant

- Ugly
- Fat
- Idiot
- Old
- Loser
- Lazy

We may *never* speak these words to describe others, at least out loud, but many of us apply these labels to ourselves *every day*. Start a tally of words like these in a little notebook for a week. You will be amazed at how many times you are tearing yourself down with these vicious thoughts.

Do you hear those words in an accusing voice? In my mind, those words are always tagged with "you are." *You are so stupid. You're too fat to wear that. You're lazy.* "You are" can be fighting words if followed by a negative. That's exactly what our enemy does. The accuser engages us in a fight against ourselves to destroy our effectiveness for God's purposes.

If Satan can engage us in daily self-criticism, his battle is half-won. He knows that if we don't see ourselves the way God sees us, we cannot fully love others the way God wants. Our husbands, children, coworkers, family members, friends, fellow Christians, and even strangers indirectly suffer from our lack of self-love. But we suffer most of all from self-criticism, because we live a life that's a shadow of the one God longs to live with us.

Susie Larson writes, "Do you know what nourishes the soul? It's knowing (and believing) that we are the object of God's intimate and powerful love."[1] What we need is a healthy view of God's love toward us, so we can love ourselves the way he calls us to do, which will then flow over onto others. We can meditate on God's Word to reprogram our self-criticism into reminders of his love, which will heal and transform us.

THE MANY FORMS OF GOD'S LOVE

Sometimes I ask my children, "Do you know that Mom loves you?" They always answer yes. Then I challenge them, "How do you know?" That's a harder question to answer, but normally it's based on what I do for them, like making meals or giving hugs.

This is how the Bible describes God's love for us. Sure, God tells us straight out that he loves us. The Bible also describes the many ways God demonstrates his love for us.

As you consider Bible verses in Christian meditation, apply them directly to yourself. Place your name inside the verse when it fits. Think of these verses as personally penned love letters to your heart. A particularly good passage for this is 1 Peter 2:9. I like the New Living Translation the best. It tells me I am chosen, royal, holy, and a precious possession, with a specific purpose of showing others God's goodness. When I say, "Sarah is . . . ," and fill in the blank with these powerful adjectives, I find peace. This single verse helps me silence critical remarks from my inner judge.

GOD LOVES YOU

Never forget that God's love for you is costly and precious. He gave up his Son for you, so you could spend eternity in heaven with him. 1 John 4:9–10 wraps us in God's loving arms. It tells us that real love cost our Father his Son, which shows how much he loved us before we were capable of returning love to him.

Jesus told his disciples to remain in his love, because he loved them just as the Father loved him (John 15:9). Ponder this deep thought: the Holy Father loves the sinless Son with perfect love. Jesus loves us with this exact kind of love, every moment of every day. We can return to this astounding love again and again through Christian meditation.

Any woman who honestly declares she loves God is secure in his love. He promises to reveal himself to you if you seek to know him with your whole heart and mind. You must pursue him actively, seeking him diligently as described in Proverbs 8:17.

Because of our sinful natures, we don't deserve to be God's daughters. Like the prodigal son in Luke 15, we tentatively return to him, thinking we'd be content only to be his slaves. But our heavenly Father welcomes us with an intimate embrace, kissing us and holding us close. He calls us his children in 1 John 3:1. Anytime you doubt your worth, you can return to this verse for affirmation of God's love for you.

GOD DELIGHTS IN YOU

When you delight in someone, you take great pleasure in their company. That's why God always watches over you, caring for you tenderly. He doesn't simply tolerate you; he chose you to be his own. He delights in you and keeps you safe (Ps. 18:19).

God directs every detail of your life—can you imagine that? Think of all the mundane day-to-day moments you experience. The ones that pass even *your* notice at times, such as when you are driving a familiar route or folding a basket of laundry. God knows those moments and treasures them, because you matter so much to him. Psalm 37:23 tells us he delights in the smallest details.

GOD SAVES YOU

Whatever battle you are facing, God is waiting for you to call on him for help, so he can save you. He is glorified when you praise him for saving you. He wants to save you from your enemies, just as he saved David from his many enemies, including King Saul (Ps. 18:3).

God patiently listens to all your prayers. When you cry for help, he is glad to save you and draw you closer to him. Your desperate cries are welcome to him. He will help you in your troubles and he's ready to be your Savior (Ps. 34:6).

GOD RESCUES YOU

Think about all the troubles you've faced in the past week, month, or year. How has God rescued you from each one? How has he grown your faith through each trial? Do you recognize the ways God has come to your rescue every time (Ps. 34:19)? Meditation can help you recall those times of rescue and invite you to trust God more.

If you're on God's team, he rescues you and keeps you safe. Nothing can come between you and God's love for you (see Rom. 8:38–39). He does not condemn you like your inner judge tries to do. He protects you as his valuable servant (Ps. 34:22).

GOD PROTECTS YOU

In the difficult days in which we live, isn't it comforting to know that we have a hiding place when we draw close to God? He is protecting you from many troubles you cannot even see in the spiritual realm. He is surrounding you with shouts of joyful deliverance in the heavenly places (Ps. 32:7).

Psalm 91:4 paints a beautiful picture of God's gentle lovingkindness. Like a mother duck brings her little ducklings under her wings in a storm, God softly covers you with faithfulness when hard times come. Picture yourself as hiding under his wings the next time you feel insecure, and he will show himself as your loving protector.

GOD UPHOLDS YOU

I love the idea of God holding me up with his strong, holy hand when I feel low. I can't lift myself out of my struggles, but God will uphold me. In troubled times, I meditate on Isaiah 41:10, which helps me rise above my troubles in God's strength, righteousness, and holiness.

When you feel desperate and cling to God in hope, your Father is holding you up in front of your enemy, showing him that he cannot snatch you out of God's hand. Psalm 63:8 also tells us that God upholds us with his right hand, the hand that fathers used to bless their children in ancient times. His right hand strongly upholds you and blesses you as his beloved child.

Are you still struggling to accept the fact that God loves you? That you are a treasure and a delight to him? If so, make it your goal in the next few weeks to meditate on verses that demonstrate God's love for you. Ponder them well. They will sink into your spirit and work their healing powers.

Remember the phrase, "If you don't have anything good to say, then don't say anything at all"? Tracie Miles says, "While this is often said in reference to what we say about others, it can also be applied to what we say about ourselves."[2] I can't agree more. In those times when you aren't feeling so great about yourself, simply don't say anything bad at all. Refocus your thoughts on praising God for how much he loves you instead.

THINK DIFFERENTLY ABOUT YOURSELF

We're living in a time when women are being more honest about the ways they harm themselves when they feel bad. I struggled with self-harm when I was a depressed teen. Every night, I picked at my face until it bled, to correct so-called imperfections. When I'm stressed out now, I'm tempted to pick again.

But I've learned to recognize my wrong behavior when it begins, call myself what God calls me in Scripture (loved, chosen, precious, etc.), and stop the destructive behavior. Even though I sometimes struggle with picking at my skin, I take care of my body the vast majority of the time. I eat, sleep, shower, and exercise.

As Ephesians 5:29 points out, I don't completely neglect my body out of hatred, and I'm sure you're the same way, no matter how much you struggle with self-criticism. When I think about Jesus caring for me in those daily essential ways, I feel sorry for the times I thought my body was unworthy of care. If he says my body is worthy of care, I must care for it. I hope this verse sparks renewed positive thinking in you too.

In my opinion, Psalm 139 is the ultimate affirmation of God's love and care for us. Psalm 139:14 tells us we are fearfully and wonderfully made. If you've ever seen an artistic masterpiece in a museum, you may have used these words to describe it. You are God's masterpiece, friend! Even if you aren't as far along as you'd like to be, you're the pinnacle of God's creation.

Chrystal Evans Hurst writes, "I've learned that my uniquely beautiful life is an original work of art designed for my good and for the glory of the One who orchestrated my existence, even if it doesn't look like it at this moment. You are allowed to be both a masterpiece and a work in progress simultaneously."[3]

Think about this quote in relation to the verse. You were a masterpiece as a baby and a girl. You are a masterpiece now, what-ever age you may be. You are still a work in progress, but God is continually renewing you as his treasured masterpiece. Can you now sincerely agree that you are fearfully and wonderfully made? I encourage you to say it out loud right now, declaring to your inner judge and to the enemy that you believe the truth about yourself, starting today.

APPLYING GOD'S LOVE TO YOUR THOUGHTS

You can speak these verses back to your inner judge and your accuser each time a self-critical thought zips through your mind. Make a vow to stop tearing yourself down.

When it comes to your body image, remember that the enemy will continually attack you in this area. Alli Worthington writes, "The enemy is a master of distracting and hurting women of God by keeping us busy hating how we look."[4] Don't let the enemy gain ground over you in this area. Commit this area to prayer, asking God to help you see your body the way he sees it, as described in Psalm 139.

If you need to get healthier, don't let your current struggle take over your thought life. You may need to make some changes so you can be the best version of the woman God called you to be. But it doesn't mean your thought life has to be sacrificed in the process. Meditate on verses that inspire you, and invite God into your journey toward better health. One of my favorites is 1 Timothy 4:8:

For physical training is of some value

God places value on physical exercise, as clearly stated in this verse. We need to do everything we can to keep our bodies healthy for God's glory. As we work to stay healthy with proper exercise, diet, rest, and self-care, we become better equipped to serve in God's work.

but godliness has value for all things

Though God values the time and effort we put into caring for our physical bodies, he cares even more about our spiritual health. We must pursue obedience, because it demonstrates our love for God and shows a picture of Jesus to the world. When we pursue godliness, it blesses every part of our lives and blesses others in the process.

holding promise for both the present life and
the life to come.

What hope! God promises here that the efforts we put into our spiritual health matter now on earth, and our efforts to pursue godliness will continue to matter even when we get to heaven. God sees everything we do, and everything we do matters to him, though we won't fully realize this until we see him face-to-face and he shows us what our pursuit of godliness has produced.

Does the mirror give you grief? For several years in our new home, we only had mirrors at medicine-cabinet level. I could handle the facial view of myself okay. When we renovated our master bath, I had to deal with the full-length mirror, which showed my hump and other issues I'd been ignoring. That's when I had to make peace with the mirror and not allow it to mock me anymore.

I like Rachel Macy Stafford's idea of how to handle the mirror: "*What would love do?* I ask myself as I look in the mirror and start picking myself apart. Love would look past the reflection and say, 'Look how far I've come.' Love would say, 'I'm grateful for another day.'"[5]

Will you start speaking words like that to yourself? Will you cover your mirror with sticky notes of Bible verses to spark meditation? You don't have to allow the mirror to condemn you. You can use that mirror to give God glory.

MORE MEDITATION VERSES

Here are a few verses from Psalm 139 for inspiration. Choose your favorite Bible version and meditate on the whole psalm.

- ∾ O LORD, you have examined my heart and know everything about me. (Ps. 139:1 NLT)

- ∾ You discern my going out and my lying down; you are familiar with all my ways. (Ps. 139:3)

- ∾ You go before me and follow me. You place your hand of blessing on my head. (Ps. 139:5 NLT)

- ∾ For you formed my inward parts; you knitted me together in my mother's womb. (Ps. 139:13 ESV)

∾ Your eyes saw my unformed body; all the days ordained for me were written in your book before one of them came to be. (Ps. 139:16)

Prayer

Father in heaven,

I praise you because you fearfully and wonderfully made me. You show your love to me in so many ways, they are impossible to count. I am amazed at your love for me.

I confess that I often think critical thoughts about myself, which are out of line with your will for me. Today I want to start replacing those thoughts with meditations on how much you love me, which will help me love myself.

Thank you for showing me new ways to think about myself. I want to change so I can love you better, treat myself right, and let your love in me overflow to others.

Give me a keen awareness of the times when I'm not speaking words of blessing over myself. Help me change from the inside out with conviction from the Holy Spirit. Renew my mind with your healing power.

In Jesus's name,
Amen.

REFLECTION QUESTIONS

1. What is your least favorite body part? How has this chapter helped you see it as good?

2. What new word can you pull from Scripture to fight against accusing thoughts? Ideas: I am God's delight, I am loved by God, God rescues me.

3. How will you redeem your time in front of the mirror?

NOTES

[1] Susie Larson, *In Over Your Head: Balance That Works When Life Doesn't* (Harvest House, 2018), Kindle version.

[2] Tracie Miles, *Love Life Again: Finding Joy When Life Is Hard* (Colorado Springs: David C. Cook, 2018), 47.

[3] Chrystal Evans Hurst, *She's Still There: Rescuing the Girl in You* (Grand Rapids: Zondervan, 2017), 28.

[4] Alli Worthington, *Fierce Faith: A Woman's Guide to Fighting Fear, Wrestling Worry, and Overcoming Anxiety* (Grand Rapids: Zondervan, 2017), 174.

[5] Rachel Macy Stafford, *Only Love Today: Reminders to Breathe More, Stress Less, and Choose Love* (Grand Rapids: Zondervan, 2017), 30.

CHAPTER FIVE

THOUGHTS THAT CRITICIZE OTHERS

*Why do you see the speck of sawdust
in your brother's eye and pay no attention
to the plank in your own eye?*

—MATTHEW 7:3

During a stressful season of childhood, I began bullying one of my classmates to the point that she considered switching schools. When my mom found out, she was shocked that her rule-following good girl had said and done such hateful things for months. Though I repented of my wrongdoing and even became good friends with the girl, I never forgot my dark ability to lash out in criticism toward someone else.

In Chapter Two, I mentioned that I'm an INFJ on the Myers-Briggs personality test. The J stands for judging. Most of the time, this means that I use my God-given discernment and reason to correctly determine what is right and what is wrong. The dark side of this strength is my constant temptation to criticize others from my self-imposed judgment seat. It's a struggle that I consider one of my main character flaws. Only through God's grace and by meditating on his Word have I been able to get a handle on it.

We live in a world that becomes more and more contentious by the day. People spout off on the Internet in ways they would never speak in person. With the proliferation of critique-based reality shows, we barely flinch anymore when someone else speaks criticism, constructive or not.

Of course, none of us like to *receive* criticism from others. It hurts! I can remember the exact words that bullies spoke to me. I can still see emails sent in all caps, virtually screaming insults at me. Those critical words from others sink deep, and we'll deal with them in the chapter on forgiveness.

If criticism hurts so much, why do we think it or offer it so freely? For me, it's due to a secret desire to feel better than others. Thoughts I nurse in self-protection. They are based on insecurity, which means I don't feel good enough about myself, so I try to put others down to feel a little bit better about myself. Nasty, icky thoughts. Hard to admit. But I am guessing you struggle with them too.

The truth is, God is the only one who can perfectly judge human hearts. I can't see into that person's heart who is giving me such trouble or committing obviously wrong acts. But God can see into his or her heart and deal with it in perfect justice. I'm learning to let God be the only one who sits on that judge's seat in my heart, when I'm tempted to think critical thoughts about myself or others. Let's allow him to transform our thinking with his truth rather than our own.

HARMFUL CRITICISM

Harmful criticism starts with critical thoughts. We deem others "too much" or "not enough." Whether their appearance or actions are morally repugnant or simply make us feel uncomfortable, we cast judgment first in our mind. Sometimes, the judgment passes through our lips or through our fingertips or bodily expressions. We must deal with our tendency to criticize others in our minds before we share our thoughts, whether they are spoken, written, or communicated in body language.

There are a thousand ways to speak truth to someone in a way that isn't harsh or critical. But this requires thoughtfulness, which can be cultivated through meditation. Let's meditate on the ways God warns us against criticizing others.

Why do you see the speck that is in your brother's eye, but do not notice the log that is in your own eye? (Matt. 7:3 ESV)

When I heard this verse as a child, it made me laugh, since hyperbole is the preferred style of humor in my family. It was as funny to me as Jesus saying that it's as hard for a greedy person to get into heaven as it is for a camel to go through the eye of a needle (Matt. 19:24). Yet I don't think Jesus wasn't trying to be comedic. He was using an extreme example to catch his listeners' attention and force them to stop and consider what they were doing.

In this passage of Matthew 7, Jesus tells us to stop judging others unless we want to be judged by the same standards. He tells us to first deal with our own problems, so we can see clearly to help others with theirs.

Jesus has a major problem with our nit-picking. To see a speck in someone's eye, you need to get really close. Unless they're inviting you to help them remove the irritation, you are invading their personal space without permission. That's the definition of being rude, and in 1 Corinthians 13 we learn that love is not rude. Love is kind.

In her book *Begin Again*, Leeana Tankersley tells a painful story of going to Target with her children after her husband had been out of town for work for several days. She was weary and frazzled but couldn't avoid the necessary trip for essentials. She admits that her kids were completely out of control, climbing the shelves and being disruptive. A woman near her began verbally lashing out about Leeana's parenting. Never looking her in the eye, the woman dumped her blistering criticism on Leeana, leaving her reeling with shame.

When her child asked her what the woman was talking about, Leeana got teary and replied, "She was being unkind."[1] Mercifully, God sent her two friends, right then and there in Target, to offer her words of comfort and affirmation.

Our unkind words slay others with criticism. When we speak those words, we aren't thinking about how our words make them feel. We're simply offloading our opinions and judgments to feel "better" inside. Like the girl I bullied in grade school, we wound others at the heart level when we spout off criticism. But we don't usually consider their feelings, while we fiercely guard and defend our own in self-protection.

Our wayward feelings and thoughts are often the log Jesus wants us to deal with first. Why did the woman cast judgment on Leeana? We don't know for sure, but she certainly must have been entertaining critical thoughts before they passed her lips.

Jen Hatmaker writes, "Folks who thrive in God's grace give grace easily, but the self-critical person becomes others-critical. We 'love' people the way we 'love' ourselves, and if we are not good enough, then no one is."[2] As we discussed in the previous chapter, we must deal with our own self-criticism and insecurities in our relationship with ourselves and with God before we can rightly deal with other people.

The Pharisees were ready to stone a woman who had been caught in adultery. When they presented her to Jesus, he told them they could cast stones, as the law allowed, if they were without sin (John 8:7). One by one, the men dropped their stones and walked away after Jesus's convicting statement. I can't throw a stone at someone when I'm dealing with the same issue. I can't sling a stone even if I'm *not* dealing with that issue, since I have my own log-sized problems to keep me busy.

The apostle James warns us against criticizing one another. He says when we criticize another believer, we are criticizing and judging God's law (James 4:11–12 NLT). When we ponder God's holiness, we can give him the full credit for being the only qualified lawgiver and judge. We have no right to take his place—we are far from qualified. If we criticize others, God sees it as criticizing his holy law. Focusing on God's holy role as judge helps us see that we are equals with other people in God's eyes.

Jesus simply told us to refrain from judging others, so we will not be judged (Luke 6:37 ESV). Simple to read; not so easy to follow. We can meditate on this verse and turn it into a prayer, asking God to help us refrain from holding on to judgment, condemnation, and unforgiveness. The phrases are short, and you can memorize them and call them to mind every time you are tempted to judge.

CONSTRUCTIVE CRITICISM

When I was an art student in college, we had weekly class critiques. Each of us would pin our designs to a wall-sized corkboard. For a whole class period, we would take turns offering observations and helpful tips.

I remember one day when my teacher pointed out that my classmate had chosen a green that was a bit too yellow. It was clashing with the reds in his design, causing his design to lose its elegance. He couldn't see it. She patiently went up to the board and pointed out the areas where his greens needed to be bluer. He replied, "But I used a blue green there."

After a brief investigation of his colored pencils, he realized the issue. "I'm color-blind," he said. "You all are probably seeing yellow green, but I see it as a blue green." Without the teacher's constructive criticism, he would not have realized how his color blindness was affecting his design and how he needed to seek feedback in his future career to make sure his designs would be pleasing to clients.

This is how constructive criticism can be a blessing. We can't always see the truth about ourselves. We need others to point out our blind spots. Others can help us grow and improve our character.

When constructive criticism is offered gently, with respect for the other person's needs, it is a blessing. Whether the person receives it as a blessing is not under our control. But we can control how and when we offer constructive criticism to others, and whether it is appropriate to offer it in the first place. That control starts in our minds, and we can grow wiser through meditation.

You don't have the right to speak truth into someone's life unless they know you care about them. Otherwise, it's pure judgment that will cause destruction. Cultivating a relationship with someone before you confront them is essential. You can ask many questions in prayer when meditating on Ephesians 4:15.

Instead, speaking the truth in love

Speaking truth and love at the same time is one of the most difficult challenges to master in the Christian life. However, with lots of practice and prayers for God's direction, we can learn to speak the truth in love. It's also important to ask others to forgive you, and to forgive yourself, when you don't get this right. Remind yourself that you are still learning, and grant yourself grace. If you tell others that you are on a quest to speak both truth and love, they will support you even when you make mistakes.

We will in all things grow up into him

As we learn how to speak the truth in love, we will experience spiritual growth. Jesus always spoke the truth, and he always spoke with love. In our learning process, we will become more like Jesus and offer more mature fruits in our spiritual walk. The ability to speak the truth in love is the mark of a mature Christian.

who is the Head, that is, Christ.

In this chapter of Ephesians, Paul is writing about the body of Christ. We are all members of this body, and Jesus Christ is the head. In order to speak the words of Jesus to others, we must strive to speak the truth in love. Look to Jesus as your example in this pursuit. Let God teach you and mature you as you meditate on this powerful verse.

Rather than tearing someone down in your mind, consider ways to build them up (1 Thess. 5:11). Always look for a positive. Think of reasons to praise rather than reasons to criticize. Pray for opportunities to speak blessing into someone's life. God will transform your thoughts so you can be an encourager instead of a critic.

PURSUING KINDNESS

Kindness is a sweet, healing balm that is undervalued in our culture. Yet it has great potential to reverse the sweeping trend of public and private criticism. When you think kind thoughts, they turn into kind words. They help transform you into responding like Christ, rather than responding like the world. Kindness serves as salt and light in your spheres of influence.

In her book *The Kindness Challenge*, Shaunti Feldhahn offers a thirty-day approach to transform your interactions with people through kindness. It includes not speaking a single negative word against the person you've designated for the challenge. This process requires a thought-life revolution first, before you speak or act. Focusing on kindness has the power to change your relationships, even the most challenging ones.

Are you surprised that the "soft" virtue of kindness has this ability? Feldhahn writes: "True kindness always strengthens and empowers, never weakens. It changes you, not just others. It melts hardness and makes gentleness immensely powerful."[3] But she admits kindness is delicate enough to be destroyed unless we practice it with intention.

I took this challenge toward a truly difficult person in my life. Even though our relationship didn't improve after those thirty days, my attitude toward her softened. I began to think compassionate thoughts toward her, because I saw how her contentious ways drove many people away. I started praying for her even though she shunned my kind words. When I moved to a different stage in my life and didn't need to interact with her anymore, I left with peace in my heart rather than bitterness. Kindness changed my attitude in a tough situation, and I'm grateful it proved more powerful than criticism.

How does kindness benefit us? It replaces our criticism with a healthy sense of control. We can't change others, but we can control our thoughts and responses toward them. In this way, we benefit ourselves and benefit others. Criticism, by contrast, is cruel and brings destruction (Prov. 11:17).

Since we are chosen and loved by God, he wants to clothe us in his beautiful robes (Col. 3:12). They are woven with threads of kindness, which is interwoven with compassion, humility, gentleness, and patience. All these lovely virtues involve blessing others rather than protecting our self-interests. Meditate on this verse, asking God to help you "wear" each of these virtues.

Critical thoughts stir up contention. When we let these thoughts escape our minds and turn into spoken words, texts, emails, or posts, quarrels may break out (2 Tim. 2:24). God calls us to a different kind of living. He wants us to show kindness without resentment, so we can freely teach others how to grow in faith. We can use this verse for meditation to become more like Jesus.

Kindness helps us make connections with people we may have criticized before. God may surprise us if we set criticism aside and give kindness a try.

I discovered this surprise through spending time with my husband's friends. They get together after work to enjoy adult beverages, tell jokes, and hash out their problems. Believe me, I'm far more comfortable hanging out with my Bible study gals than these rough-and-tumble, worldly guys. However, they have become dear to me since I decided to treat them with kindness rather than suspicion and nit-picking.

I've spent a lot of time thinking about how much criticism Jesus faced. He lived a life contrary to what people expected, but he lived the life God called him to live, so he was bulletproof against criticism. He showed kindness to people considered outsiders— women, prostitutes, cheaters, drunkards, and lepers. The Son of God spoke his harshest words of criticism against religious people who set themselves up as judges—those who run in *my* circles today. Meditating on verses about kindness, compassion, and loving others has melted away the hard edges of the J in my personality, which stands more for Jesus than Judge now.

I want to be a connector like Jesus was. Malcolm Gladwell describes connectors as unique facilitators of ideas in our social structure. He says: "[Connectors] don't see the same world that the rest of us see. They see possibility, and while most of us are busily choosing whom we would like to know, and rejecting the people who don't look right or who live out near the airport, or whom we haven't seen in sixty-five years, [connectors] like them all."[4]

I don't know if I'll ever reach that level, because the I stands for Introvert in my personality. But I can strive to be more like connectors by thinking kind thoughts rather than critical ones. You can too.

MORE MEDITATION VERSES

- Kind words are like honey; sweet to the soul and healthy for the body. (Prov. 16:24 NLT)

- Your love for one another will prove to the world that you are my disciples. (John 13:35 NLT)

- This is my commandment: Love each other in the same way I have loved you. (John 15:12 NLT)

- Above all, love each other deeply, because love covers over a multitude of sins. (1 Pet. 4:8)

- Whoever claims to love God yet hates a brother or sister is a liar. (1 John 4:20a)

Prayer

Father in heaven,

I praise you because you show me kindness. You don't criticize me, but you lovingly correct me when necessary. You are the perfect teacher for showing me how to treat others.

I confess that I think unkind thoughts toward others, and sometimes I carry them over into words and actions. I'm sorry for the times I hurt others with criticism. Clean my heart and mind from toxic habits of faultfinding, suspicion, and cruelty toward others.

Thank you for giving me hope that I can change. Thank you, Jesus, for providing many examples of how to speak the truth in love.

Teach me how to replace criticism with kindness. Start the transformation in my heart and mind, then carry it over into my actions, words, and body language. Show me how to make new connections with those I may have criticized before.

In Jesus's name,
Amen.

REFLECTION QUESTIONS

1. In what ways are you most tempted to criticize others?

2. What are the roots of your criticism of others? Did you see it modeled as you grew up? Did others criticize you? Pray that God will remove that root from your heart so you can heal.

3. Which verses will you use to instantly fight off critical thoughts of others?

NOTES

[1] Leeana Tankersley, *Begin Again: The Brave Practice of Releasing Hurt and Receiving Rest* (Revell, 2018), Kindle edition.

[2] Jen Hatmaker, *For the Love: Fighting for Grace in a World of Impossible Standards* (Nashville: Nelson Books, 2015), xv.

[3] Shaunti Feldhahn, *The Kindness Challenge: Thirty Days to Improve Any Relationship* (Colorado Springs: Waterbrook, 2016), 17.

[4] Malcolm Gladwell, *The Tipping Point: How Little Things Can Make a Big Difference* (Boston: Little, Brown and Company, 2002), 53.

CHAPTER SIX

FEARFUL THOUGHTS

*There is no fear in love,
but perfect love casts out fear.*

—1 JOHN 4:18 (ESV)

T he fear of abandonment has haunted me all my life as a child of divorce. Even though I was only four years old at the time, I vividly remember the day my father left. I knew something was wrong when I saw him crying for the first time ever. Then I saw the suitcase in his hand. A claw of terror gripped at my throat and silenced me as he hugged me goodbye.

As he drove away, my deepest fear took hold and never let go. It has colored every relationship I've ever had with a male. In the back of my mind, I'm always thinking, *He's going to leave you someday.*

For the most part as a teen and young woman, I kept boys at a distance, though I longed for their attention. In my senior year of college, frustration and loneliness haunted me daily. I drove to the banks of the Tennessee River with my Bible, asking God to give me a verse to relieve my pressure. By those peaceful waters, I opened my Bible to Hebrews 13:5b, which reads, "I will never leave you nor forsake you" (ESV). The powerful verse didn't completely heal me that day, but God used it as a seed planted in my thoughts that slowly took root.

When my husband and I were newly married a couple of years later, the fear of abandonment tightened its grip. My husband was late coming home from work one day. Panic rose in my chest a half hour after his normal arrival time. I called his cell phone, but he didn't answer. I called his workplace, but the secretary told me he was long gone.

Pacing the floor while glancing at the clock, I worried that he had been in a wreck and was unable to call for help. Though I felt ashamed of my hysteria, I called the sheriff's office to report my husband missing. The person on the other end of the line tried to calm me with placating words. Then my husband pulled into the drive, and I hung up. I clung to him, wetting his shirt with my tears.

He was bewildered by my dramatic reaction. We fought about it. As we argued, he told me over and over, "I'm not your dad." Though it wasn't a positive conversation, God used it to get my attention. I started attending counseling to deal with my fear that had spilled over into my marriage. Years passed before I lived like I believed the truth God revealed to me by the river: he is the only One who will never leave me.

After almost two decades of marriage, those wild, panicked thoughts still run through my mind at vulnerable moments, especially when my husband hasn't called to say he'll be late. My mind still goes right to the ditch, thinking he's lying there, dying, never to return home. But every time those fears haunt me, I repeat that verse to myself: "*I will never leave you nor forsake you.*" Even if a worst-case scenario plays out someday, God will still be with me, and I've learned to trust him with my fears through meditating on Hebrews 13:5b.

I wish that the fear of abandonment was the only one to haunt me. For example, I fear carnival rides, and it's not from lack of trying. When I rode the Tilt-a-Whirl in middle school, I screamed bloody murder the whole time, and the ride operator had to pry my fingers off the bar one by one since I was too panicked to get up after it was over.

My children tease me for not attempting anything riskier than the lazy river at the water park. They ask if they were being held ransom unless I slid down the biggest water slide, would I do it? I say, "Absolutely *not*." Someone else will need to rescue them, because the idea of going down that sharp-angle slide is 100 percent terrifying, 0 percent enjoyable for me.

What are your fears, friend? I know you have a few haunting you. I'm guessing your oldest fears have to do with deep hurts, like my fear of abandonment. Maybe you struggle with fears for your children or your marriage. Maybe you have fears about your career or your finances. Maybe health is connected to your worst fears. Perhaps rejection is your number one fear. No matter what fear haunts you, God will help you overcome it with courage. You can cultivate courage through Christian meditation.

FACING OUR DEEPEST FEARS

Whatever your deepest fear is, God wants to help you face it. He doesn't want it haunting you for years. He wants to quiet your fear with his loving presence. Our theme verse will help you face your deepest fear and draw close to God.

> *There is no fear in love, but perfect love casts out fear.*
> (1 John 4:18a ESV)

In the chapter on self-criticism, we talked about pursuing God's love as an antidote. When we are secure in his love, our fears are quieted, because God himself is love.

Since my deepest fear is connected with my father, I have specifically worked on developing trust in my perfect heavenly Father, who will never let me down. When I am afraid, I go to my bed and imagine climbing into his lap and letting him hold me. In that safe place, I meditate on the truths in his Word, and my fears subside. There, I find perfect peace and love, which heals all my fear-ridden thoughts.

I know many of you reading this also have wounds associated with your father. I know how hard it is to trust your heavenly Father when your earthly father destroyed your trust. But if you choose verses that speak about God's kindness and faithfulness as your Father and meditate on them regularly, the Holy Spirit will begin to restore your broken trust.

If you suffer from the fear of abandonment like I do, Psalm 27:10 may feel like it was personally written for you. It states that even if your parents abandon you, God holds you close. Let God use it as a healing balm for your fear through regular meditation.

Though earthly fathers sometimes forsake their children, God steps in as Father to all who are abandoned. He is high and holy, yet he is close to you because you are precious to him. He defines himself as your Father and defender in Psalm 68:5.

If you have been abandoned, you may feel like a slave to fear. Why do slaves live in fear? Because punishment always looms if they aren't performing up to standard. This is not how your heavenly Father is. He is a loving Father who brings you into his own family, and he loves hearing you call him Daddy (Rom. 8:15 NLT).

Even if your deepest fear isn't the fear of abandonment, meditating on verses about God as your Father can help you face your fears with greater courage. Knowing that God is bigger than your fear can give you peace in the scariest times. Believing that God controls the terms of your deepest fear can help you relax in his loving arms. Trusting that God has a plan and purpose for you despite your fear can help you find hope.

CONQUERING OUR FEARS

When I was young, my sister and I went to a family friend's home after school. She and the youngest boy of the family loved to play in the field behind the house. To play in the field, they had to climb over the gate.

My fear of heights prevented me from climbing. They would beg me to come play, but I started trembling when I tried to swing my leg over the top of the gate. Embarrassed, I stepped down, went back inside, and read my books, feeling trapped by my fear.

Our fears limit us. They hold us captive. They steal possibilities away from us. In our own strength, we can't overcome our worst fears. But with God's help, we can conquer them.

Psalm 18 is one of my favorite Bible passages to center me when I feel afraid. Verse 29 tells us that with God's strength we can scale a wall and crush an army (NLT).

When I think of scaling a wall, I think about how easily a lizard can scurry up my garage wall when it catches a glimpse of me. With no fear at all, the little lizard climbs crazy heights. Even though I'm too afraid to climb over a gate, much less scale a wall, God has helped me over many emotional walls that I once thought impossible to conquer. In his strength alone, we can cast our fears aside and shimmy up whatever wall we're facing.

Maria Furlough faced a fearful situation when her unborn baby was diagnosed with a fatal condition. He was predicted to live only a few hours after birth. She had to fight her choking fear every moment while she carried little Gideon in her womb. She says: "Our fears are not trustworthy. They are not based on truth, they do not know facts, and they are guilty of vast exaggeration. Our fears do not love us, they do not care for us, they take no account of our pain or our sorrow. Our fears are unworthy of our attention. They do not deserve the deepest parts of us, nor do they deserve our attention or our allegiance."

She also says, "We know and can be assured that even if our worst fears come true, we have hope, compassion, faithfulness, newness, and provision from a God who does not lie to us."[1]

Even if the walls of your fears are closing in on you, you can trust God to help you conquer your fears. He will provide the supernatural strength and endurance to free you from the fear that threatens harm.

When your fears feel like walls around you, you can turn to the book of Isaiah for help. In Isaiah 35:4 NLT, we learn that God is coming to destroy our enemies and save us. Remember in Chapter One when we talked about the spiritual battle? God will destroy any power of the enemy over you. He will save you from spiritual attacks. You don't need to give in to fear, because God is fighting your battles for you.

Did you know that God promises to hold your hand when you are afraid? (See Isa. 41:13.) When I was a depressed teen, my mom encouraged me to ask Jesus to hold my hand at the beginning of the school day and to remember he was holding it throughout the day. Even though I felt a little silly doing it, I pretended Jesus was walking around holding my hand, and I gained comfort knowing he was near me in my trials. In times when you face trials and fear threatens, you can ask Jesus to hold your hand too.

God never promises to completely remove our fearful situations. But he does promise to be present with us through them and protect us when we pass through them (Isa. 43:1–2). Whether we face overwhelming floods of troubles or burning flames of trials, he is by our side. His promises are based on his intimate relationship with us as our Shepherd and Redeemer.

PURSUING COURAGE

We can focus on courage when our fears threaten. Lynn Cowell defines courage as "the strength to go forward *even* in the face of fear. . . . Alone, we don't possess confidence, courage, or bravery. He is forming this fortitude where there has been a void, where it never has existed before."[2]

Jesus sometimes asks us to step out of our comfort zones and join him in a journey that requires us to pass through fear. Late one night his disciples were in a boat on the Sea of Galilee. Jesus came walking to them on the water, and they were understandably shaken. But Jesus told them, "Take courage! It is I. Don't be afraid" (Matt. 14:27).

When Peter said he wanted to walk out on the water, Jesus called him. Peter walked on water for a few moments but lost courage when he saw the wind and waves. When he began to sink, Jesus reached out his hand and rescued Peter, pulling him safely back into the boat.

How long would Peter have walked on the water if he had kept his focus on Jesus? We don't know. Yet Jesus would have allowed Peter to experience more of his power if he hadn't given in to his fear.

Is Jesus calling you out in the midst of your fear to do something new that feels scary? Do you hear him telling you to take courage and keep your eyes fixed on him? If so, your fear may not subside until you obey. You may need to walk right through it to get where Jesus is calling you.

Jennie Allen says, "Jesus isn't scolding us for being afraid; He is calling us out of our comfortable boats to do something unthinkable, something that is possible only with His power."[3] What is he calling you to do that requires you to take courage?

When I need courage, I turn to one of the most familiar psalms that Christians love: Psalm 23. I slowly meditate on verse four and gain peace, strength and courage from it.

> *Even though I walk through the valley*
> *of the shadow of death*

Which valleys have you walked through in your life? Each valley is darker because the shadow of death looms over it. Whether it was a sickness of a loved one, dark nights in your marriage, or the impending death of long-held dreams, you had to walk through the valley. I know how scary and unsafe that feels. Those valleys are where the enemy loves to tempt us to give into our fears.

> *I will fear no evil, for you are with me*

Because God is with us in every single one of our valleys, we can fear no evil. The enemy will have his weapons ready in the valleys; you can count on that. However, we don't have to give into fear, because Jesus is walking right alongside us in those valleys. His strong, loving presence will guide us through.

> *your rod and your staff, they comfort me.*

Psalm 23 describes the Lord as a good shepherd. A shepherd uses his staff and rod to protect sheep from predators. When you are fighting off fear while walking in the valley, remember that the rod and staff of God's Word is protecting you from defeat. You can gain great comfort by meditating on God's Word as you face fear in your valleys.

After the Israelites had wandered the desert for forty years and Moses had died, it was time for Joshua to move God's people into the Promised Land. Not only were the people afraid of the inhabitants of the land; they were afraid of change. I wouldn't consider wandering around in the desert to be comfortable, but it is what they knew. They didn't realize how much better the Promised Land would be, since it was unfamiliar. Like the Israelites, we resist change and shrink back in fear rather than stepping forward in courage.

God knew the bridge between the desert and the Promised Land was called Courage. He told Joshua over and over to "be strong and very courageous." God also said, "Be careful to obey all the law my servant Moses gave you; do not turn from it to the right or to the left, that you may be successful wherever you go" (Josh. 1:7). God will show us the right path to take as we step forward in courage.

Sometimes courage also requires waiting. When you're afraid, waiting is the last thing you want to do. You simply want the fearful situation to be over with! But God can use the waiting period to build your faith. Psalm 27:14 tells us we must be strong and take heart while we are waiting for the Lord. Your courage can grow as you wait for God to relieve you from your fears.

We can have courage even during suffering because Jesus has already won the ultimate victory for us (John 16:33). When I faced marriage trials that had unknown endings, I had to look my fear of abandonment in the eye and realize that Jesus had already won the battle for me. He didn't take my suffering away, but he gave me peace in the middle of it and built my courage in the process.

Sue Detweiler says, "You may not feel 100 percent free from fear, but little by little, as you step out in faith, you will see God work miracles in your life."[4] You can step out in faith by meditating on God's Word as you face your fears. Jesus may even ask you to walk on water with him so he gets more glory and you gain more courage.

MORE MEDITATION VERSES

- The LORD is my light and my salvation—whom shall I fear? The LORD is the stronghold of my life— of whom shall I be afraid? (Ps. 27:1)

- God is our refuge and strength, always ready to help in times of trouble. So we will not fear when earth-quakes come and the mountains crumble into the sea. (Ps. 46:1–2 NLT)

- When I am afraid, I put my trust in you. (Ps. 56:3 ESV)

- For God has not given us a spirit of fear and timidity, but of power, love, and self-discipline. (2 Tim. 1:7 NLT)

Prayer

Father in heaven,

I praise you because you are completely trustworthy. You are perfect love, and there is no fear in your presence. I am glad I can always feel safe with you.

I confess that too often, I let fear take control of my life. I let fear limit my choices and steal my opportunities. My fear keeps me from living the life of faith you want me to live. Free me from the bondage of my fears, Lord, especially my oldest fears that you know better than I do.

Thank you for granting me courage to overcome my fears. Thank you, Jesus, for winning the ultimate victory for me. I don't have to face my fears alone, and I thank you for always walking beside me.

Help me to choose courage, based on my faith in you, when I feel afraid. Inspire me to trust you more every day so that my faith is stronger and my courage grows. Show me where my lack of faith is holding me back and break down the strongholds of fear in my heart.

In Jesus's name,
Amen.

REFLECTION QUESTIONS

1. What is your deepest, oldest fear?

2. How do you typically handle your fears? How will you change your method to deepen your trust in God?

3. What verses will you memorize to fight off fears when they arise?

NOTES

[1] Maria Furlough, *Breaking the Fear Cycle: How to Find Peace for Your Anxious Heart* (Grand Rapids: Revell, 2018), 47.

[2] Lynn Cowell, *Make Your Move: Finding Unshakable Confidence Despite Your Fears and Failures* (Nashville: Thomas Nelson, 2017), 12.

[3] Jennie Allen, *Nothing to Prove: Why We Can Stop Trying So Hard* (New York: Waterbrook, 2017), 155.

[4] Detweiler, *Women Who Move Mountains*, 31.

CHAPTER SEVEN

IDOLATROUS THOUGHTS

Their land is full of idols; they bow down to the work of their hands, to what their fingers have made.

—ISAIAH 2:8

For years I had a big, beautiful idol. But I didn't know it. I thought it was only a necessity. But in time, God showed me how it had taken a place in my heart that only he could fill.

My husband is a builder. His first major project was our house. As newlyweds, we spent weekends driving on county roads, looking for the exact right spot to build. Eight fully wooded acres became available in the same area where my ancestors had settled from Germany four generations before. The country church across the street was required to offer it to the list of interested buyers. My grandpa had first rights of refusal, but it had to be passed over by several other families before we got a chance at it.

As I sat in our tiny apartment, I prayed like crazy. I had never wanted something so badly before. The property was located a mile from my family's farm. As a teen, I had dreamed about living in the country. I wanted the honeysuckle-scented air, the owl sounds in the night, and the gorgeous sunsets. I wanted the peace you can't find when living in town.

The farm also represented security to me. As a child of divorce, I could always count on my great-grandparents and my grandparents being there for me, when family chaos swirled around me. Many warm memories from my happy times in the country could now be replayed in my own future family.

We got a phone call with an offer, which we quickly accepted. Hooray! For months, we cleared trees and brush by hand. I carried many two-by-sixteen boards to the site where my husband built the concrete forms for the foundation. I helped tar the walls and lay the wood flooring until I was too pregnant to bend over or carry things. With the help of our family and friends, we did everything other than the HVAC and drywall. We felt so proud, like pioneers charting new territory.

When we moved in on July 4, 2004, we had a new baby boy and nearly half our appraised value in sweat equity. I stood looking out the large windows in the living room with 12-foot ceilings, marveling at the lush woods and praising God for his goodness.

My husband started to work longer hours, building spec homes as a side business. Because I was already a homebody by nature, my house became a fortress when loneliness set in. As more marriage and family problems unfolded in the years that followed, I retreated more often into the walls inside the woods, sometimes not leaving for four or five days.

One day my husband came home at the far edge of his frustration. He wanted to quit his job and go out on his own. I asked him to give me one day to pray about it, and I began a liquid fast since I was still nursing my baby. I went upstairs to my main sanctuary in our home, the master bedroom, where I so often cried and prayed and wrote my heart on journal pages. It was a sacred place where I met with God most often.

I got down on my knees in front of the picture window, folding my hands atop the cedar chest that had belonged to my parents before their divorce. Looking into the spring woods with the bright green leaves just beginning to open on the hickories and maples, I prayed, "God, show us your will about his job." I began crying in fear of the future, secretly worrying about having to move if our finances drastically changed.

I heard God's still, small voice as clearly as if he were standing next to me: "Put all the trust you have in this house in me." Then the heavens closed.

I was bewildered. I had intended to fast and pray about my husband's career, but then God spoke to me about my house. What did that mean?

That message kept following me, though I resisted it. It started haunting me in songs and sermons on the radio. Verses about idol worship began standing out to me in Bible study. Finally, I broke down when I listened to a CD of Andy Stanley's teachings that mentioned contemporary idol worship, which brought me to my knees again in my bedroom. Through many tears, I admitted to God that I had made my house an idol. I had sought it first for stability, comfort, and security rather than God. I committed to choosing him first when I was tempted to choose the house. In my bravest and hardest step of faith, I surrendered the house to God to do with as he pleased.

That was about ten years ago, and we're still in this house. It is a precious gift, but it is no longer an idol in my heart. God gently showed me in his Word that I could find eternal security in him rather than in my big, beautiful idol. I still praise him in our living-room-turned-cathedral. But I hold it more lightly now, appreciating it every day, yet worshipping the Lord God Almighty instead of worshipping a lovely conglomeration of wood, glass, and cement.

CONTEMPORARY IDOL WORSHIP

Your idol may not be as obvious as mine. Maybe your idol is small and shiny, a smartphone you simply can't put down. Maybe it's a son or daughter or grandchild who consumes your time and energy to the detriment of your marriage. You may idolize a television show, exercise class, closet of clothes, wine after work, romantic relationship, or any number of other good things that sit on your heart's throne instead of God. As you read this chapter, ask God to reveal the idols you may not even recognize.

Idol worship today is sophisticated and sneaky. The enemy uses subversive tactics to dress idols up as innocent playthings or justifiable needs, rather than reveal their devastating potential. Like the beautiful fruit on the tree of the knowledge of good and evil, our idols have the appearance of doing us good, helping and sustaining us. They can't be all that bad, right?

Jennifer Dukes Lee writes: "At the root of idolatry is the cunning twisting of truth. Cool gifts from God—like sex, food, and even happiness—become nooses slipped around our spiritual necks. The enemy convinces us that anything God made is better in excess."[1] Look for areas of excess in your life, and you'll soon find your idol.

Scripture describes how idol worship ushers suffering into our hearts and strife into our relationship with God. It's clear that God takes idol worship seriously and considers it lethal for our spiritual health. By meditating on verses about idolatry, we can uncover the truth about the place idols have in our hearts and start tearing them down, one by one.

When we prioritize something or someone over God, we arouse his jealousy (Deut. 32:16). Our jealousy is sinful, but God's jealousy is holy. He wants our hearts to belong to him and no one else, and when we choose an idol instead of him, he burns with anger and heartache. Think about how you would feel if your beloved chose someone else over you; that's how God feels when you choose an idol.

God longs for a face-to-face relationship with each one of his followers. Our idols strip away that relationship. We turn our backs on God when we choose idols; he doesn't turn his back on us (1 Kings 14:9b). But we anger and offend him with choices that may seem unimportant or excusable to us. He knows when we are worshipping idols instead of worshipping him.

Idols can become snares to us (Ps. 106:36). Have you ever walked into a spiderweb? I've done so in my woods, and it's an awful feeling trying to remove the nearly invisible threads while wondering if a spider is about to bite you. Walking into a spiderweb can be a shock. Idol worship also snares us, one indulgence at a time. Before we know it, we are in service to an idol that is wrapped all around our hearts. It can unexpectedly bite us before we wake up and realize how far we are from God.

God sometimes uses blunt language to help us wake up to the truth about idol worship. Idols are worthless and cause us to become worthless (Jer. 2:5b). Worthless in service to others. Powerless to bless others. Hopeless in relationship to God. The more power we give our idols, the more isolated and cut off from the body of Christ we become. That's the enemy's end goal—to keep us far away from God and others. If an idol can help him accomplish that goal, he'll make it as enticing as possible.

Our idol worship breaks God's heart. God freely offers us his love. Yet when we cling to idols as our primary source of comfort or provision, we reject God's love (Jon. 2:8). Notice the love thread running underneath all the warnings in these verses. Consider God's great love for you when he prompts you to destroy the idols in your heart. He's there waiting to replace them with his boundless love.

RENOUNCING IDOLS

Getting rid of idols isn't an easy task. The enemy will engage in hand-to-hand combat as you work to tear them down. But the Bible promises blessings to you as you begin the process.

Admitting that your idols cannot provide for you is the first step in letting them go. Place your hope in God instead when you are tempted to turn to your idol for comfort, and he will show you the riches of his provisions. He will show you how your idols are empty and vain, but he can be trusted to meet your needs (Jer. 14:22).

When you are tempted to beat yourself up for turning back to your idol, you can find great hope in Ezekiel 36:25–27:

> *I will sprinkle clean water on you, and you will be clean;*
> *I will cleanse you from all your impurities and*
> *from all your idols.*

Worshipping idols makes us unclean in God's eyes. But God promises to cleanse us from our tendency to worship idols. We can't possibly do all the work of cleansing ourselves, because our sinful hearts will always lean toward idol worship. The fact that God promises to cleanse you can be a comfort to you.

> *I will give you a new heart and put a new spirit in you;*

God promises to provide us with a new heart and new spirit when we commit ourselves to worshipping him alone. He will turn your heart and spirit toward him once you have sought cleansing from your idol worship. This passage of Scripture is a great source of hope.

> *I will remove from you your heart of stone and*
> *give you a heart of flesh.*

The longer you worship an idol, the harder your heart becomes to the things of God. But if your heart is soft, like a baby's skin, it is sensitive to God's promptings. You can turn this sentence into a daily prayer in your quest to be idol-free. Ask God to turn your stony ways into softness, and he will delight in answering your prayer.

> *And I will put my Spirit in you and move you to follow*
> *my decrees and be careful to keep my laws.*

When we turn from idols, we have the Holy Spirit's help in fighting off temptation to return to them. As you study and meditate on God's Word, the Holy Spirit will remind you of God's righteous requirements. You will become more like Jesus as you carefully pursue God's will instead of giving your heart over to idols.

In your quest to remove idols from your heart and mind, it's good to be aggressive. We can't be casual about removing idols. We must be deliberate. Break, smash, cut down or burn your idol; make a permanent change (Deut. 7:5). Do whatever is needed to completely remove the idol's power from your life. Ask God for discernment. He may allow you to keep it but change your attitude, like he did with my house. He may also ask you to give it up completely, and if he leads you to do so, trust and obey.

Since we live in a decadent culture, it's essential for us to continually turn away from the things of this world. If your idol is materialism, meditate on 1 Timothy 6:17 before you go shopping, even if it's simply to a rummage sale. We all have a trace of the idol of materialism in our hearts, and it's good to regularly bump it off the throne through meditation.

DEVOTING YOUR HEART TO GOD

Trusting an unseen God with your whole heart isn't easy. But I've learned it is the only life worth living.

As a child of divorce, I had an insatiable need for relationships. I took whatever I could get, toxic or healthy, to fill my needs, even as a Christian. Over time, God began stripping away those relationships and helping me understand how I had made idols of my family and friends. I could see, hear, touch, and smell them. I couldn't do that with God.

Elisabeth Elliot wrote, "If we hold tightly to anything given to us, unwilling to let it go when the time comes to let it go or unwilling to allow it to be used as the Giver means it to be used, we stunt the growth of the soul."[2] I had to admit that my soul wasn't growing when I attached my heart's desires to what I could experience through my senses.

When my relationships suffered, I sought a real relationship with God for the first time. I still can't see, hear, touch, or smell God. But because I've spent years drawing closer to him through his Word, he is more real to me now than my "real" life. I can't wait to "hear" his voice and interact with him through the day. However, I had to set aside everything else in my heart, including my family, to get to this point in my faith. Jesus made Matthew 10:37–39 come alive in my heart and mind:

If you love your father or mother more than you love me,
you are not worthy of being mine

When I was in fourth grade, my pastor would sometimes lead our religion classes on Fridays. I remember a particular day when he covered this verse. That night, I cried out to God in prayer. I said, "Lord, I don't think I love you more than my mommy or daddy—yet. But I want to love you more. Will you help me?" God used this verse to reorient my heart toward him, even when I was still a child. He can use it to reform the focus of your love as well.

> *or if you love your son or daughter more than me,*
> *you are not worthy of being mine.*

When each of my three children was born, I fell head over heels in love. I couldn't imagine letting them go, and they needed me so much. Over the years, I have regularly tuned in to Focus on the Family radio broadcasts as a work-from-home mom. These broadcasts taught me to hold my children loosely, because they first belonged to God and were simply my gifts to steward well. As they have grown, I have learned to not make my children into idols and surrender them back to God's care.

> *If you refuse to take up your cross and follow me,*
> *you are not worthy of being mine.*

Life is just plain hard sometimes. It can feel like a heavy burden to carry. However, Jesus tells us that we must take ownership of our lives and carry our responsibilities. He promises to help us carry our burdens (Matt. 11:28–30), but it's important to him that we are intentional in carrying the loads he has assigned to our care. If we don't do this, we risk falling from his favor.

> *If you cling to your life, you will lose it;*
> *but if you give up your life for me, you will find it.*

This is a great paradox of the Christian faith. We must surrender all that is valuable to us—even our closest relationships and dearest possessions—to live a life pleasing to God.

To find the abundant life God promises for us, we must fully devote our hearts to him. Devotion to God dethrones the idols in our hearts. Devotion requires faithfulness, a daily cultivation of relationship through meditation, study, prayer, and worship. I promise that the more devoted you are to following God, the less idols will appeal to you.

The Lord's servant Ezra was a teacher of God's Word, and the Lord's hand was on him. He enjoyed a close relationship with God because he devoted himself to the study and observation of God's law (Ezra 7:1–10). Studying and observing God's law are keys to living a life devoted to God. The most devoted followers of God I've known have one thing in common: a commitment to regular study of his Word. We can enjoy a closer relationship with God as we devote ourselves to studying and meditating on God's Word.

Another key to the devoted life is worshipping God in the fellowship of other believers. The members of the early church were devoted to fellowship, listening to the disciples' teachings, praying and eating together (Acts 2:42). Your local church will help you stay devoted in your walk with God through accountability and teaching. I highly recommend connecting with a local church this week; it will make a huge impact on your faith.

A natural outflow of our devotion is service and love for other people. Your local church gives you immediate opportunities to serve others in love. God never intended for you to be alone. He wants you to demonstrate your devotion to him in service to others. Romans 12:10 tells us to be devoted in love, putting others above ourselves. Your local church is the perfect place to start putting this verse into practice.

The Bible also tells us to be devoted in prayer (Col. 4:2). Prayer is an ongoing conversation with God you can have from the moment you wake up until you close your eyes for sleep. As you develop a habit of prayer, your heart's devotion to God will grow deep roots. Your prayers can be full of thanksgiving and praise while you watch for God's answers.

Devotion to God will help you make better choices (Titus 2:12). Since I've gotten serious about my faith, I don't miss my idols anymore. The sinful pleasures aren't as enticing as they used to be. As you destroy your idols and choose to be devoted to God, he will transform your heart into the likeness of Jesus, who lived a life of total devotion to his Father's will.

MORE MEDITATION VERSES

- Do not turn to idols or make metal gods for yourselves. I am the LORD your God. (Lev. 19:4)

- Do not turn away after useless idols. They can do you no good, nor can they rescue you, because they are useless. (1 Sam. 12:21)

- Protect me, for I am devoted to you. Save me, for I serve you and trust you. You are my God. (Ps. 86:2 NLT)

- "I am the LORD; that is my name! I will not give my glory to anyone else. I will not share my praise with carved idols." (Isa. 42:8 NLT)

- What agreement is there between the temple of God and idols? For we are the temple of the living God. As God has said: "I will live with them and walk among them, and I will be their God, and they will be my people." (2 Cor. 6:16)

Prayer

Father in heaven,

I praise you for your majesty. No one is higher than you. No one deserves glory and praise but you. You are my source of security, comfort, provision, and hope. Nothing else compares to you.

I confess that I have allowed idols to overtake your rightful place of lordship in my heart. Some of my idols are careless choices that have never been good for me. Other idols are wonderful gifts you've given me that I elevate too highly. I am sorry that I choose to put anything above you, for everything is yours. Help me to worship you as the Creator of all things, rather than worshipping what you have created.

Thank you for cleansing and purifying me of my sins. Thank you for offering yourself to me. I am grateful that you don't turn your back on me forever, Lord. You welcome me when I come to you with a humble, repentant heart.

I ask you to show me all the idols standing in the way of a deeper relationship with you. Help me remove them, Lord. I want to devote my heart to you rather than anything else, even the good gifts you give me. I trust you will bless me both now and in heaven for seating you on the throne of my heart.

In Jesus's name,
Amen.

REFLECTION QUESTIONS

1. After reading this chapter, which idol is obvious to you? Which one is newly apparent?

2. Why is it hard for you to put God on the throne of your heart instead of your idol?

3. What can you do differently this week to show devotion to God?

NOTES

[1] Jennifer Dukes Lee, *The Happiness Dare: Pursuing Your Heart's Deepest, Holiest, and Most Vulnerable Desire* (Carol Stream, IL: Tyndale Momentum, 2016), 13.

[2] Elisabeth Elliot, *Passion and Purity: Learning to Bring Your Love Life under Christ's Control* (Grand Rapids: Fleming H. Revell, 1984), 162–63.

CHAPTER EIGHT

GUILTY THOUGHTS

My guilt has overwhelmed me
like a burden too heavy to bear.

—PSALM 38:4

F or years guilt haunted me like ghosts. Real guilt over problems I caused and people I hurt. False guilt over embarrassing
situations and words that needed no apology. So many guilt ghosts
wandered through my mind daily, I couldn't tell the difference
between the real ones and the false ones. They all had accusing
faces, sternly staring with eyebrows raised and hands on hips.
Each one taunted me, saying, *You're bad. You're a fake. You're fool-*
ing everyone.

Every guilty moment, false or real, had a guilt ghost attached.
The enemy used my photographic memory against me, bringing
up several ghosts every day, unbidden. Memories from twenty or

thirty years ago surfaced along with a unique and menacing guilt ghost trailing behind each one, waiting to be loosed.

One guilt ghost that refused to leave me rose up from an incident in a grade school classroom. I waited too long to use the bathroom and had an accident in the middle of class. The ghost collected hard evidence of my guilt in the moments that quickly followed. Warmth spread down my legs into a puddle on the tile floor. The teacher's stern lips pressed together in disdain. Mocking laughter from every child in the classroom. A too-long mop handle I couldn't wield well enough to clean up my mess, so the janitor had to take over. Dusty clothes and too-big shoes from the lost-and-found box that I had to wear the rest of the day. The suspended silence at recess, when classmates whispered about me while I scooted around the edges of the gravel, not daring to make eye contact with them. A wet bag of underwear stuffed in the bottom of my bookbag, which I would be forced to explain to my mom.

Hard evidence. Hard to refute—so many witnesses. Hard to justify—I was old enough to know when I needed to get up and go. The guilt ghost shoved in beside me on the bus ride home, like an older bully I didn't have the strength to push out of my seat. It battered me, just like the condemning thoughts I was fighting so hard that year as a child of divorce. I was trying and failing to weather the upheaval I hadn't asked for, and that incident held spectacular proof. The guilt ghost breathed foul odors on me while it snarled, *You're a mess. You're a nuisance. You're unwanted.*

The ghost of that memory haunted me for decades. Every time I felt unwanted, I was instantly transported back into the classroom, with the smell, rejection, judgment, and isolation all returning as if the incriminating incident had happened the afternoon before. The enemy sent that guilt ghost and many others to keep me from claiming my true identity in Christ: a beloved princess held in highest esteem.

Guilt ghosts haunted me when I looked at objects I had taken without permission. Even the sight of a paper clip or cheap pen would taunt me while assaulting me: *You're a thief.*

If I saw someone years after I'd been in a Bible study where I had overshared, I froze. The guilt ghost put a hand over my mouth to keep me from saying hello with freedom, then punched me in the gut: *You're a loser.*

The biggest, meanest guilt ghost punished me when I looked back at the year 2000, when my husband and I met and married within eight months. Those wild months when I rebelled for the first time in my life. I jumped into infatuation's embrace to soothe all the pain of my past and felt the grip of guilt instead, because we lived together before we married. For five, ten, fifteen years afterward in our rocky marriage, I faced that guilt monster every morning when I glimpsed our wedding photo on the dresser. The monster-ghost was much bigger than me, and he always won our standoff with his left hooks. *You're damaged goods,* he said every time he socked me.

These ghosts heaped pile after pile of guilty layers on me. No one knew that I was haunted, but I'm sure they knew I was weighed down. Some people said, "I don't know how you do so much." Others said, "You're at church almost every day, aren't you?" I had to stay busy to keep the guilt ghosts away. Keep moving so I could dodge their insults and assaults. When I was alone and at my weakest, they did their dirtiest work.

In 2006, a friend invited me to join Bible Study Fellowship. That year we studied the book of Romans. When I was looking at the crown jewel of Romans 8, God kept calling me back to verse 1: *There is no condemnation.*

God wanted me to be free from my haunting past guilt. Since Jesus had died for all my sins—past, present, and future—I had nothing to fear. No guilt ghosts could conquer me, because Jesus had already won the victory for me. God wanted me to see that he no longer condemned me in my guilt for the real sins, and he had *never* condemned me for my words or actions that generated false guilt. He wanted me to find freedom in Christ alone.

The Holy Spirit started reminding me of that verse when the ghosts crept up on me. If I said out loud or in my mind, "There is no condemnation for me now," the ghosts slunk away. I repeated Romans 8:1 hundreds of times to fight off those ghosts. Especially the biggest, meanest ghost: he needed to hear it most often. Every time I said it, he shrank a little bit. Now he's about the size of a wasp, which I can swat rather easily.

The guilt ghosts don't haunt me regularly anymore. They probably won't ever completely go away. But if they show up, I will send them away with the truth of God's Word.

THE IMPORTANCE OF CONFESSION AND REPENTANCE

I grew up in a church denomination with a liturgical service, which follows a predictable pattern every Sunday. First, we sing a song of worship, then confession immediately follows. The rest of the service progresses in a beautiful pattern of readings, hymns, and prayers that draws me back into communion with God.

A danger lies in saying the same prayers and creeds over and over again, because our minds can disengage and the words can lose their meaning. However, the value I gained from saying the same confessional prayer for many years is that I have it ready to go when real guilt shows up, and it reorients me to right standing with God.

For example, when I snap at my children, I'm tempted to beat myself up even after I've apologized to them and they have expressed forgiveness. When the guilt ghost knocks on my door, I can chase it away by meditating on that familiar, Scripture-based prayer.

In the prayer I confess that I am sinful by nature and my sins create a barrier between me and God. I confess that my thoughts, words, and actions are wrong, and that I have not loved God, myself, or others in a healthy way. I admit that I deserve punishment rather than mercy, but I ask God's forgiveness based on Jesus's sacrifice. At the end, I ask God to help me learn from my mistakes and help me get on the right path without taking guilt along.

I put this verse into action when I make a confession, and God's forgiveness washes over me like a refreshing waterfall:

> *Then I acknowledged my sin to you and did not cover up my iniquity. I said, "I will confess my transgressions to the* LORD." *And you forgave the guilt of my sin.* (Ps. 32:5)

Confession is the first half of the bridge between guilt and freedom in Christ. The other half of the bridge is repentance. That's a word that means to turn in the opposite direction. It's not enough simply to confess your sin. To be free from guilt, you must turn in a different direction and do the opposite action to get on the right track.

To free ourselves from all our guilt ghosts, we must commit our sins to daily confession. We must ask the Holy Spirit to reveal our known and unknown sins on a regular basis and commit to keeping a short account with God. As soon as the Holy Spirit reveals a sin, confess it and form an action plan for repentance. Think of the virtue on the opposite side of the vice and find a verse for it. Then meditate on it and pursue righteousness.

HANDLING TRUE GUILT

True guilt over real sins will make us feel awful. Psalm 38 vividly describes how guilt can affect us like a sickness affects our bodies. It's like having a burning rash with oozing wounds, complete with a fever that leaves you weak and groaning. I've only felt that way once, after getting sun poisoning while visiting the Alabama beachfront. My pale, sensitive skin experienced an overdose of ultraviolet rays, and I broke out in a full-body rash with blisters. I lay inside writhing and groaning in pain until the Benadryl finally kicked in. If my true guilt made me feel that bad on the outside, I'd confess it faster for relief.

David's colorful words in Psalm 38 are an apt description of what true guilt does to our souls. It makes our souls sick and weak, unable to recover on our own. Only God's healing touch can remove our guilt and help us move forward.

Normally, we won't confess our guilt until we feel consequences for our actions. Maybe you get pulled over for speeding and are forced to pay a fine before you start watching the speedometer (ask me how I know). Perhaps your spouse withdraws in hurt after you were harsh. Your offended coworker isn't as chatty with you, your child is in a funk, or your relative won't return your calls. These are all signs of unconfessed sin that make us uncomfortable until we set things right.

Expect the Holy Spirit to ping you in your conscience when you feel true guilt. The more in tune your conscience is with God's will, the stronger those holy pings will feel and the sooner they will convict your spirit. God disciplines you like a loving father by giving you consequences for your sinful actions. A father who wants you back in his arms.

Have you ever thought about the blessing that guilty feelings bring? Our guilt is a sign of sorrow over breaking communion with God. Deep down, we don't like to feel out of touch with God, especially when we've known the comfort and joy of being close to him. Like it did for Adam and Eve, our sin causes us to hide from God's presence because we know we've erected a barrier of sin between us and our holy Father.

Emily P. Freeman describes our guilt this way:

> We turn around and see a faraway God, hands on hips, staring at us. And we believe we have to make our way across all the ungracious territory that we have just traveled through in order to get to him. And then we wonder why we drag our feet getting there. It is impossible to retrace those steps. *What if I can't re-create the mess to get back to God?*[1]

Do you allow your guilt ghosts to keep haunting you so that you stay trapped in condemnation, fearful that you aren't worthy of saving? Do you keep rehearsing your past scenarios of guilt, confessing them hundreds of times, because you feel you must earn God's favor by sewing all those fig leaves together in several layers of flimsy covering?

When God went searching for Adam and Eve in the garden, he already knew where they were. He already knows your sin too. But he still invites you to walk with him, just like he wanted Adam and Eve to walk with him again. He offers you healing and intimacy when you confess. Don't hide from him anymore. Don't blame someone else, including God. Simply confess your sin and let his loving presence comfort you.

Meditate on Psalm 38 to decide if you're dealing with true guilt. Allow God's Word to move you to confess your sins and repent of them. The weight of your sin will be lifted as you turn your true guilt over to God, and your fellowship with him will be restored.

HANDLING FALSE GUILT

If you're like me, you beat yourself up over guilt that isn't linked to true sins. Maybe they are simply social mishaps or honest mistakes that need no confession, but you treat them like heinous crimes, dragging yourself over the coals as your condemning inner judge watches in approval.

When I was a freshman in college, I took flute lessons from a music professor. He asked me to play in one of the university orchestra's evening performances. I practiced the piece with the orchestra just one time. No one told me the dress code.

The performance night arrived. Everyone else in the orchestra was dressed all in black except me, glowing in my unwanted spotlight of a white sweater. I could have bailed after the embarrassing warm-up when my peers snickered at me. I could have made a quick run to Target for a black top to match the group. But because I didn't want to disappoint my teacher or break my commitment, I played the fool.

Weighed down with shame, I sprained my ankle as I fell down an unlit backstage stairwell, rather than exiting in front of the crowd. I cried frustrated tears as I limped in pain toward my car that night.

But I caused myself far more mental pain by replaying that false-guilt-ridden night hundreds of times in the future, allowing the accuser to hold me in his grip.

There's a fine line between true guilt and false guilt, because Satan sets out to confuse us. He doesn't want us to confess and repent of true sins, because that restores our fellowship with God. So, he tries to trip us up over confessing things that were never wrong in the first place (or confessing true sins thousands of times). This is one of the easiest ways the enemy gains ground in the battlefield of our thought lives.

Your mind can't tell the difference between false guilt triggers and true guilt triggers. Both will make you feel miserable and weak. The only way to break the power of false guilt is to meditate on God's Word and use it as your standard of truth. The Ten Commandments are a great standard, as well as what Jesus said:

> "Love the Lord your God with all your heart and with all your soul and with all your mind." This is the first and greatest commandment. And the second is like it: "Love your neighbor as yourself." All the Law and the Prophets hang on these two commandments." (Matt. 22:37–40)

If your action failed to show love to God, yourself, or your neighbors, you need to confess and repent. If your action didn't breach that standard, you have no sin to confess, and you must ask God to help you banish the false guilt ghost when it taps on your shoulder.

FREEDOM IN CHRIST

Do you remember a time of feeling free, even if it was just for a day, a week, or a season? When I was a junior in college, I transferred to a new school on top of a Georgia mountain. The mountains reached their pinnacle of beauty in October. My roommate and I spent one perfect Saturday in Cloudland Canyon, surrounded by a brilliant multicolored tapestry of God's glory. We hiked down to see a waterfall, and perfect peace stole over me while I marveled at the sight. That afternoon, I felt completely free from all my pressures and worries. I simply reveled in God's presence.

My guilt tempts me to forget about the freedom Jesus abundantly provides. When my guilt haunts me, he is waiting for me to turn to him instead. He's saying, "Remember that freedom you felt in my presence? It's available every moment of every day, because I set you free once and for all on the cross."

The enemy wants to separate us from Jesus's presence through the condemnation of guilt. But we can stand firm in our freedom in Christ by meditating when guilt threatens. Meditation verses will serve as arrows in our arsenal in our war against guilt ghosts. Let's look closely at Galatians 5:1 to gain a greater understanding of freedom.

It is for freedom that Christ has set us free.

Jesus endured suffering and shame on the cross to set you free. He was beaten, mocked, spat upon, stripped naked, and pierced for you, so that you would not need to pay the penalty for your sins. His death and resurrection set you free from sin's condemnation. He offers you freedom every time guilt threatens to shame you. Look for him holding freedom out to you in his nail-pierced hands.

Stand firm, then, and do not let yourselves be
burdened again by a yoke of slavery.

Since Jesus has already paid the price to set you free, he does not want you to burden yourself as if you were a slave to guilt. You have a choice: Will you allow yourself to be burdened by the yoke of guilt, as if you were a slave to it? Or will you choose the freedom that cost Jesus so much, which he offers to you without strings attached? Every time you feel the ghosts of guilt creeping up on you, meditate on this verse to stand firm in the freedom Jesus has already provided.

When we devote ourselves to God's Word through study and meditation, we will find freedom from the burden of guilt. As you devote yourself to daily intake of Scripture (Ps. 119:45 NLT), the path of freedom will unfold in front of you. You can walk in the freedom of God's presence, delighting in his glory. Guilt won't weigh you down on that path when God's Word is guiding your heart.

One of the Holy Spirit's many roles is to remind us of our freedom in Christ (2 Cor. 3:17). You can ask him to personally direct you when guilt threatens. Ask him to ping your spirit and trust him to offer you freedom every time guilt weighs on you. Pray that he will help you find lasting freedom as you develop your relationship with God.

God's Word gives us that freedom. When my children were infants, I sought out the best parenting advice I could find. I remember reading an article by James Dobson, who said the most well-adjusted children have firm boundaries yet plenty of freedom to explore. I learned that when I set parameters around their play areas, their imagination thrived since they felt secure.

God's law works the same way for us. The perfect law gives us the boundaries for our freedom in Christ (James 1:25). Your guilt is a response to the boundaries God set not *against* your freedom, but *for* it. When you intently study those boundaries and walk a life path with God's law as your guardrails, you will feel both secure and free.

MORE MEDITATION VERSES

- ꙮ But I confess my sins; I am deeply sorry for what I have done. (Ps. 38:18 NLT)

- ꙮ People who cover over their sins will not prosper. But if they confess and forsake them, they will receive mercy. (Prov. 28:13 NLT)

- ꙮ With [a live coal] he touched my mouth and said, "See, this has touched your lips; your guilt is taken away and your sin atoned for." (Isa. 6:7)

- ꙮ Let us draw near to God with a sincere heart and with the full assurance that faith brings, having our hearts sprinkled to cleanse us from a guilty conscience and having our bodies washed with pure water. (Heb. 10:22).

∿ For whoever keeps the whole law and yet stumbles at just one point is guilty of breaking all of it. (James 2:10)

Prayer

Father in heaven,

I praise you for offering me freedom from my guilt. By sending your Son Jesus to die for my sins, I truly have perfect freedom right now. You could have simply condemned me for my sins, but you provided an eternal solution. You are always worthy of praise, for this reason and many others.

I confess that my guilt has often stood in the way of my relationship with you and others. Sometimes I ignore the good guilt you give me, and my sins fester and cause additional pain. At other times I continue to chain myself to sins you have long forgiven or beat myself up for acts you never called sin in the first place. Today I confess that I am a sinner in need of grace.

Thank you for giving me your Word as my guide. Thank you that I can find freedom from my guilt through confession and meditation.

I need your help sorting out my guilt, Lord. Teach me the difference between true guilt and false guilt in my life. Help me keep a short account with you through daily confession. Ping my spirit when I need to get back on track. Shape my thought life to reflect your goodness, Lord.

In Jesus's name,
Amen.

REFLECTION QUESTIONS

1. When it comes to true guilt, do you struggle more with a
    stubborn refusal to confess and repent, or beating yourself up
    over and over for old sins? Why do you think that is?

2. Regarding false guilt, what is your biggest guilt ghost? How
    can you shrink it with the truth in God's Word?

3. If you pursued freedom in Christ every day, how would your
    struggle with guilt be different? What verse can you meditate
    on this week to help you walk a path of freedom?

NOTE

[1] Emily P. Freeman, *Grace for the Good Girl: Letting Go of the Try-Hard Life*
(Grand Rapids: Revell, 2011), 187.

CHAPTER NINE

DISCONTENT THOUGHTS

But godliness with contentment is great gain.

—1 TIMOTHY 6:6

Oh, social media, how I love you, yet you stir up something sour in me at times. You have taught me better than anyone else about my hidden tendencies to crave what others have. Their trendy clothing and jewels, perfectly highlighted hair with no frizz, and dream vacations in exotic locales keep me drooling for more than I already have. Following their feeds, I so easily forget how much abundance surrounds me in a giant feast.

As a work-from-home mom, I truly adore hopping on Facebook every morning. I treasure the photos, comments, and messages from real-life friends—it's my primary way of staying connected with the outside world through the week. No one loves a face-to-face meeting more than me—just ask my Bible study friends, who know I never run out of talking topics. Our Thursday night meetings are one of my weekly highlights. But both in person and online, I've been surprised at how often discontentment has sneaked into my thoughts.

My Facebook feed has challenged me to sincerely be happy for those who have what I don't have. It's easy to forget the trade-offs I willingly make and steep myself in self-pity. For example, we have a big, beautiful home in the country, but our sizeable mortgage means we take fewer vacations than most of our peers. I'm perfectly content with that fact until I see others' family pics from Florida or Hawaii or Costa Rica. Then suddenly the cracks in the ceiling and the scratches in the wood floor look more obvious to me, and discontentment creeps in like a low-lying fog.

Most of the women in my weekly Bible study are older than me. Their finances are more stable, and their cars are nicer. They seem less concerned about what other people think than I do in my fourth decade of life. When we were first getting to know each other, I thought they had it made compared to me. As I've learned more about them, however, I've discovered that they struggle with discontentment too.

They worry more about health than I do, and they still worry about their adult children. They are concerned about finances for other reasons—will they have enough to last at the lifestyle level they want? These dear women aren't 100 percent satisfied with their life situations or relationships. We frequently discuss how to deal with our different levels of discontentment and how to appreciate what we have. I'm learning that no matter what life stage I reach and no matter how much abundance I accumulate, discontentment will always be waiting to tempt me.

My friend Deb Wolf wrote an interesting post that has given me much-needed perspective on my discontentment. Read this excerpt and find where you stand:

If the world were one hundred people, thirty would always have enough to eat. Fifty would be malnourished, twenty would be undernourished, and one would be dying of starvation. Forty people live in a country designated as "free," twelve live in a war zone, and sixty can't speak [or] act according to their faith and conscience due to harassment, imprisonment, torture or death. Forty-five people have a computer and forty have an internet connection; seven have a college degree and twelve are unable to read. Ten people have no safe, clean water to drink and thirty-three live without basic sanitation.[1]

I'm guessing you're in nearly all of those "luxury" categories if you are reading this book. This list is not meant to shame you or me. It's meant to drive us to our knees to thank God for everything we take for granted: shelter, indoor plumbing, clean water, healthy food, electricity, Internet connection, education, and freedom. After writing this, I'm thanking him for my rural Internet connection which is slower than I like, but at least I'm in the top 40 percent of the whole world. Please put this book down for a moment and thank God for his untold abundance to you.

THE ROOT OF DISCONTENTMENT

We must be careful what we set our eyes and ears upon, because they are the doorways for discontentment to enter our thoughts. The ads we see, the social media posts we view, and the commercials we hear all tempt us to crave more. They purposely stir our dissatisfaction, so we will be moved to make a purchase. I know this from working in advertising for years. There's nothing wrong with the ads themselves; it's how we handle them that matters.

They can either feed our discontentment or move us toward gratitude for what we already have.

Comparing our lives with others feeds discontentment. I can relate to Asaph's lament in Psalm 73, when he complains that proud and wicked people seem to dodge harm and prosper with no retribution. The life of a God-follower wasn't easy then, and it certainly isn't easy now. Asaph envied their life of ease and riches in comparison to his presumably simpler life of faith.

I appreciate the raw honesty in this psalm. How often have you found yourself putting on the same attitude in comparison? How often have you looked at someone else's life and said, "They've got it easy, and I've got it hard"? God's Word gives us a glimpse of this common struggle.

Asaph admits to the Lord that his heart, burdened with discontent, had turned bitter and senseless. When he returned to fellowship with God, he saw the truth: "Whom have I in heaven but you? I desire you more than anything on earth" (Psalm 73:25 NLT).

Asaph's desire was no longer for the worldly lifestyle of the pagans. In God's sanctuary, he meditated on the truth that the end of the wicked is destruction. Since Asaph followed God, he had abundant peace, strength, provision, and protection. He desired a relationship with God more than a comfortable, safe life. I envision Asaph bowing his head while meditating in the temple, casting off his worldly desires and trusting God with the desires of his heart.

Maybe it's not the lives of others that stir up discontentment in you. Maybe you feel like God himself has shortchanged you or withheld good from you. Consider this quote from Priscilla Shirer: "We've set our expectations according to a set of flesh-based parameters crafted primarily on the basis of our own interests and desires, expecting His priorities to naturally fall in line. And when they don't, we can sometimes still find ourselves in the angry crowd, more eager to accuse Him than acclaim Him."[2]

You can be real with God about your discontentment, just like Asaph. Is God himself at the center of your desires? If not, you have room to grow. You can retrain your discontented thinking through meditation, which will reduce your cravings for things that don't last, relationships that constantly change, and wealth that can fly away at a moment's notice. Only God can perfectly meet the cravings of your heart. Let's take a closer look at Psalm 37:4 to discover how God does this.

Take delight in the LORD

What delights you? If you delight in temporary things, you will be discontent all the time. If you learn to shift your main delight to the Lord himself, you will never run out of contentment. This is the key to living a countercultural life, where discontentment threatens us on a daily basis.

and he will give you

God promises to give us not only what we need, but what we delight in. When we delight in him, we delight in his attributes. Goodness, strength, peace, and loving kindness are only a sampling of God's attributes. If you delight in these attributes that are long-lasting, your contentment level can grow. He is willing to give you everything you want if your delight is in the right place.

the desires of your heart.

God challenged me to put this verse to the test. He asked me to lay out my heart's desires to him, one by one. Then he showed me how I can seek him for the ultimate fulfillment of all those desires, as long as my main source of delight is in relationship with him. Over time, I have stopped seeking the desires of my heart in the world and started asking him to fill them. Not once have I regretted making that switch, and neither will you.

When I feel discontent in my financial situation, relationships, or other areas, I meditate on Psalm 37:4. I recommit that area to God and remind myself that seeking him is what will ultimately satisfy me. I stop the comparison game and fix my eyes on what God wants for me. Just like Asaph, we need to be honest with God about our desires and then turn to him for the fulfillment of all those desires, rather than trusting in the world to meet them. He will reward us with greater peace when we delight in him.

HANDLING DISCONTENTMENT THROUGH MEDITATION

Jerry Bridges writes in *Respectable Sins*, "We are so used to responding to difficult circumstances with anxiety, frustration, or discontentment that we consider them normal reactions to the varying vicissitudes of life."[3] Reacting to unpleasant situations with discontentment is a human reaction, not a godly response. We can take the higher road by retraining our minds with Christian meditation.

Working hard yet constantly striving for more is the American way. But it's making us miserable. We live in a heavily addicted, overweight, stressed-out culture that is desperate for peace. Our constant striving is meaningless (Eccles. 4:8), but God promises contentment when we delight ourselves in him instead of our wealth.

Not everyone who follows God will be wealthy in the eyes of the world. However, they can prosper and be content spiritually because they are depending on God to meet all their needs, as described in Job 36:11. Obedience and service to God create a contented life.

God encourages us in Psalm 131:2 to draw near in dependence upon him. When my babies were young, they calmed immediately once they were close to me. They enjoyed snuggling with me and reading books or doing finger plays. They were at their most content when I was near. He will tenderly and gently care for us when we still ourselves and seek his presence. The near space with God is where he teaches you about contentment.

The apostle Paul tells us in Philippians 4:11–13 that contentment can be learned. He wrote most of his letters while in prison, which looked nothing like the sanitized and orderly prisons of today. He was content writing the epistles with chains around his feet in a dirty, smelly Roman cell, because he knew God was ever present, and his delight was in the Lord.

When Paul was a Pharisee, he enjoyed the high life. The Pharisees controlled the coffers, and they lived like the upper middle-class members of our culture. But after becoming a Christian, Paul was often mistreated, homeless, hungry, and cold. Yet his secret of living a content life lay in his relationship with Jesus. He trusted Jesus to give him strength to face every situation, and we can do the same.

The love of money is often a stumbling block in our pursuit of contentment. Vigilantly guard your heart against the desire to get rich. Don't think that winning the lottery or gaining an inheritance will solve all your problems. Every time you are tempted by such thoughts, meditate on 1 Timothy 6:8–10. Remind yourself that you can be content with simple food and clothing, and trust God to provide all the rest.

PURSUING THANKSGIVING

God calls us to pursue contentment, and we can arrive at contentment through cultivating thanksgiving every day in Christian meditation.

When I recently saw a Peanuts "happy journal" online, I simply had to have it (plus, I had free shipping *and* a coupon). This whimsical journal calls up the young Snoopy devotee in me, who loved to list all her birthday and Christmas gifts in purple ink. Most of my journals hold painful thoughts and memories, but this one is only for the good stuff. My lists include perfectly ripe strawberries, kind words from friends, fun outings with my children, and times the Holy Spirit sent the ideal book or song to me in masterful timing. When I record those things I'm thankful for, my pen catapults discontentment miles away.

When I find a verse that sparks gratitude, I record it in my happy journal as well. Writing that verse seals it in my memory and provides a shield against discontentment.

Ann Voskamp writes, "Thanksgiving is inherent to a true salvation experience; thanksgiving is necessary to live the well, whole, *fullest* life."[4] When we offer our gratitude and thanksgiving to God, we are choosing a fuller, richer life with more heavenly blessings than earthly blessings. A life of peace and contentment, no matter how much we have or don't have.

Jesus modeled thankfulness for us. In front of a giant crowd he was about to feed, Jesus made sure to give thanks (John 6:11). God calls us to be more like Jesus every day, which includes being thankful for everything we receive. He wants us to be thankful at mealtimes and all other times of the day, whether we have a simple meal of loaves and fishes or a sumptuous feast.

The Bible doesn't tell us to be false in our thankfulness, pasting on a sugary smile when life gets tough. Look up 1 Thessalonians 5:18 and pay special attention to the phrase "in all circumstances"— not "for all circumstances." We can be thankful *in* all circumstances, abundant or sparse, because God wills us to be thankful just as Jesus was thankful. The more we practice thankfulness, the more we will become like our Savior.

Receiving a tough situation with gratitude is a mark of spiritual maturity. We can choose to look for the good in whatever situation God gives us (1 Tim. 4:4). We can fight off discontentment by remembering that everything we receive first passes through God's hands. Nothing is outside of his knowledge or provision; everything in our lives is ordained by him. Thanksgiving is an act of submission that helps us connect more deeply with God and builds our trust in him.

Our thanks to God should be both private and public. We can point the world to Jesus through our thankfulness, telling others of the good things he has done for us (1 Chron. 16:8). No matter what troubles we are facing, we can always thank God for his greatness and his wonderful deeds.

Our thanksgiving is an opportunity to be a witness to others in our culture of discontent. Go against the culture and speak with gratitude rather than complaint. Consider it a way to shine light into the darkness, which brings life and health to the places where the enemy tries to stake claims. By thanking God in front of others, we are representatives of Jesus (Col. 3:17 NLT).

MORE MEDITATION VERSES

- Then I will praise God's name with singing, and I will honor him with thanksgiving. (Ps. 69:30 NLT)

- Enter his gates with thanksgiving, and his courts with praise. Give thanks to him; bless his name. (Ps. 100:4 ESV)

- With my mouth I will greatly extol the LORD; in the great throng of worshippers I will praise him. (Ps. 109:30)

- The fear of the LORD leads to life; then one rests content, untouched by trouble. (Prov. 19:23)

- Keep your life free from love of money and be content with what you have. (Heb. 13:5a ESV)

❧ Yet true religion with contentment is great wealth.
(1 Tim. 6:6 NLT)

❧ For everything in the world—the lust of the flesh,
the lust of the eyes, and the pride of life—comes not
from the Father but from the world. (1 John 2:16)

Prayer

Father in heaven,

*I praise you for your goodness and greatness. You need nothing,
yet you choose me to be your daughter. You share all you have with
me. You are eager to pour out blessings upon me, both here on earth
and when I get to heaven. You are so good to me, Father.*

*I confess that I often feel discontent, even though I have so many
blessings. I often compare myself to those who have more than me,
which stirs discontentment. My eyes are often fixed on the shiny, new,
beautiful things of the world instead of being fixed on the wonders
and treasures available in my relationship with you. I am sorry for
putting more value on the temporal than the eternal. I want to grow
in gratitude for the abundance you have already provided me.*

*Thank you for every gift, small and large, you have provided.
Thank you for the blessings you have given me at every stage of my
life. As a sinner, I don't deserve them, but because you are good, you
keep providing them.*

*I want to become a woman who is content in every situation.
Teach me to keep track of my blessings, Lord. When I am tempted
toward discontent, flash a blessing in my mind so my heart is drawn
right back to you. Give me a hunger and thirst for things that will
last beyond this life so that discontentment is replaced with gratitude.*

In Jesus's name,
Amen.

REFLECTION QUESTIONS

1. In what area of life do you struggle most with discontentment?

2. When are you most tempted to compare your situation with the situations of others?

3. What will you do differently this week to cultivate gratitude every day?

NOTES

[1] Deb Wolf, "50 Ways to Show Gratitude to the People in Your Life," *Counting My Blessings* (blog), November 16, 2016, https://countingmyblessings.com /show-gratitude-to-people.

[2] Priscilla Shirer, *Awaken: 90 Days with the God Who Speaks* (Nashville: B&H Publishing Group, 2017), 304.

[3] Jerry Bridges, *Respectable Sins: Confronting the Sins We Tolerate* (Colorado Springs: Navpress, 2007), 73.

[4] Ann Voskamp, *One Thousand Gifts: A Dare to Live Fully Right Where You Are* (Grand Rapids: Zondervan, 2010), 39.

CHAPTER TEN

IMPURE THOUGHTS

Create in me a pure heart, O God,
and renew a steadfast spirit within me.

—PSALM 51:10

When my children were young, we loved going to the district fair together. One of their favorite spots was the state's conservation department booth. They got to pet turtles and see real snakes in glass cages. My boys oohed and aahed at the giant catfish swimming in a forty-foot tank. I still remember a simple display in a pure white plastic bin. The conservation agent handed us magnifying glasses to look at the tiny organisms swimming in water taken from a pond, just like the one in our own backyard. We saw bits, flecks, and squiggly creatures that weren't visible to the naked eye.

"See that one?" the agent said as he pointed to a teeny water worm. "If you drink pond water, this one will make you retch like you've never done before. It might even land you in the hospital for dehydration." I used his warning to instruct my boys to never take a sip from our pond, since the invisible impurities could sicken them to the point of death.

Our impure thoughts are invisible, but they sicken us terribly and lead us on a path to destruction. We live in a sex-saturated culture, and even happily married Christian women secretly struggle with lust. I wish I could say it hasn't affected me, but it has. In our post-Christian, pleasure-driven world, we must use the fine sieve of God's Word to filter impure thoughts from our minds, since temptation comes at us nonstop. Nothing else will be as effective as the living power of Scripture to cleanse impurities from our thoughts.

When I came home from college on holiday breaks in the late 1990s, I enjoyed taking a break from my studies by flipping through catalogues and magazines my mom had saved for me. I'm an artist, and I love looking at beautiful things. The Williams-Sonoma catalogue helped me dream of smart ways to fill my future kitchen, and the Ballard Designs catalogue whisked me away to the French countryside. The Spiegel catalogue inspired me to pretend I was a fashionista who could wear designer clothing, and the Victoria's Secret catalogue took me into pleasurable, dangerous territory.

Those women were gorgeous from head to toe, and the lingerie was lovely. Tempting. Seductive. Which color of lace would I like best? Which silky thing would look prettiest on me? Before I realized it, I had spent forty-five minutes gazing at the women. I had fallen into the velvet-lined trap of soft porn without even knowing what I was doing.

I feel a little sick and dirty just writing that. But I know I'm not the only one who struggles with impure thoughts, especially those that come without my hunting for them.

I looked at those Victoria's Secret catalogues in the days before porn was widely available on the Internet. Now porn is at our fingertips whether we seek it or not. Recently I searched for a Bible app. In the suggestion list, an icon of a bent-over busty girl in stilettos advertised another (obviously not Bible) app. Who would expect to find porn there?

The enemy is insidious, and he instructs his followers to know just what to do to hook you. This year I watched a Proverbs 31 Ministries video on YouTube for an online Bible study. In the multi-paned YouTube screen that always pops up at the end, my eyes were naturally drawn by the magnet of a striking image. A teenage girl with short black hair, pale skin, and dark eyes looked to her left. As an art student, I was trained to use the high contrast between black and white to move the viewer's eye, and that's the technique the designer used on the image. Her eyes pointed to the next pane on the right, where a graphic sex scene was pictured in miniature. After a Proverbs 31 Ministries video!

The enemy knew *exactly* what he was doing there. He lured someone from the porn industry to place their dirty images right after God's Word was delivered. He directed someone to place that busty bent-over girl in the algorithm for a Bible app search. Friend, if we don't guard our minds against impurity, we will get sucked into a deadly vortex without even trying. Our willpower isn't strong enough to fight it, because our flesh will always lean toward impurity. Perhaps no other thought-life area is more important to fight with Christian meditation than this one.

DEALING WITH IMPURE THOUGHTS

The first step to dealing with impure thoughts is to admit that we have them because we are human, we have eyes, and we are prone to sin. If we don't admit that impure thoughts happen to us and we deny their power, shame can cover our minds in such a thick layer that the enemy will have already won the battle. Starting today, resolve to be honest with God when impure thoughts enter your mind. The temptation itself is not a sin, but entertaining the thought can quickly lead to lust. Turn the impure thoughts over to him every time, and he will drastically decrease the level of the battle you face.

Next, we must identify our triggers and diligently avoid them. You may be tempted by movie or television stars, famous musicians, professional sports players, or other celebrities. Romance novels may be a downfall for you. Internet porn could be a snare. Or you may be entertaining a secret crush on a coworker, delivery person, or even a fellow church member. Be ruthless in evaluating yourself, asking God to point a spotlight at the triggers that tempt you most. Confess your sin and commit to repentance. Then prayerfully enact barriers that will regulate how often you expose yourself to the triggers. Make dramatic changes, if necessary, to stop the flow of impurity.

Another way to keep impure thoughts from entering your mind is to "bounce" your eyes away from the trigger, the same as you would immediately pull your hand away from a hot stove.[1] Bouncing your eyes means not lingering on an image; immediately looking away breaks the chemical rush of pleasure in our brains that makes us crave more impurity. If sexy commercials or racy Internet images pop up in your view, force your eyes to look away in the same second. The enemy's arrows will be deflected, and you will honor God's command to "flee from sexual immorality," as described in 1 Corinthians 6:18.

Take inventory of how you feel in the moments when you are most tempted toward impurity. For me, the base feeling is loneliness. Think about healthy ways to deal with the base feeling that don't involve impure thoughts. When I'm tempted, I take a walk, sing along with praise music, call a friend, or get involved in a project like weeding the garden or cooking supper. You need to have a bank of healthy activities to redirect you if impure thoughts are a common temptation. Pray about the base feeling and seek God's comfort and strength so that impure thoughts aren't such a draw in your moments of weakness.

Remember that the enemy will double or triple his attacks when you commit to removing impure thoughts from your mind. Expect the temptations to increase as you begin to transform your thinking. Tearing down strongholds requires extra spiritual strength, which you can find in Christian meditation.

HANDLING IMPURITY WITH MEDITATION

Donna Partow writes, "The more we see God for who he is—the more we behold his holiness—the more we will see our *need of cleansing*."[2] By meditating on what the Bible says about God's purity in contrast to our impurities, we can come clean before him.

It's important to remember that only the blood of Jesus can cleanse us from our sins. Our willpower isn't strong enough to rid us of impure thoughts. None of us can say that we are clean from our sins apart from Jesus (Prov. 20:9). Only a close dependence upon Jesus, moment by moment, can purify our hearts and minds.

God wants to reward your pursuit of purity by showing you the loveliness of his purity (2 Sam. 22:27). When you choose impurity, you choose to set up a barrier between you and your heavenly Father. Your pursuit of purity is a way to cultivate a deeper relationship with God and enjoy a new side of him you may not have appreciated before.

God invites us to commune with him. But he wants our hearts and minds to be purified before we seek a deeper relationship with him (Ps. 24:3–4). This is why you must vigilantly guard your mind against impure thoughts; they block your fellowship with God and reduce the quality of your spiritual life.

You can guard your mind from impure thoughts by meditating on God's laws. I enjoy meditating on Psalm 19:7–9 to elevate my view of God's laws.

The law of the LORD is perfect, refreshing the soul.

Who doesn't need a dose of refreshment? The perfection of God's law cuts through the imperfection of everything else, including our impure thoughts. His laws are a breath of fresh air to our minds and hearts. By focusing on the perfection of God's laws, your thought life will be refreshed.

The statutes of the LORD are trustworthy,
making wise the simple.

We can trust that God's laws are perfect, never changing, and always reliable. They are powerful enough for even simpleminded people to understand. His laws grant us wisdom, which gives us peace. Knowing that God's laws are trustworthy can help us feel secure.

The precepts of the LORD are right, giving joy to the heart.

Since our impure thoughts lead us astray, we can right ourselves by thinking about God's precepts. If you've been on the wrong path for a while, the rightness of God's law will feel refreshing and new. This newness of life, available through God's Word, will bring joy to your heart.

The commands of the LORD are radiant,
giving light to the eyes.

The sun has the most radiant light in our world. It's so bright that we cannot look directly at it. The commands of God's Word are even more radiant. They light up our eyes to see our impure thoughts in a new way. When God's Word shines light on our impurities, we can be cleansed by him.

The fear of the LORD is pure, enduring forever.

A reverent fear of God is essential for Christian living. God considers our reverence for him to be pure and lasting. When you read God's laws, approach them with a healthy fear of God's holiness, power, majesty, and justice. Your impure thoughts will fade when you embrace a healthy fear of God.

*The decrees of the LORD are firm, and
all of them are righteous.*

The stronger the hold impurity has on your thought life, the more you should meditate on God's laws to break the enemy's stronghold. Developing a love for God's laws through Christian meditation will make impurity seem far less appealing than it used to be. As you meditate on the righteousness of his decrees, you will understand that your impure thoughts don't belong in your life.

Memorize the prayer in Psalm 51:10 for the moments when you slip and fall into impurity. We will never be completely immune to the enemy's power, and he loves getting his hooks in our tender flesh. Refuse to condemn yourself. Instead, use the beautiful prayer in Psalm 51:10 to seek God's cleansing and recommit your mind and heart to him. As you regularly meditate on it, the Holy Spirit will use this verse to guard and purify your heart and mind.

God shares the riches of his goodness with those who seek purity in him, as described in Psalm 73:1. If you want the best God has to offer, you must commit your thoughts to purity. But be honest with God about your impure thoughts that need to be replaced. He sees every impure thought that you entertain and every base feeling that craves impurity as a solution (Prov. 16:2).

Nothing you think escapes his notice. However, when you align your motives with God's will, you have nothing to fear.

Matthew 5:8 is a simple yet profound verse. Only those who desire to have a pure heart will see God face to face someday. They are the ones who will enjoy the most intimate relationship with him now and in heaven. If you want a more intimate relationship with God, you must make purity of mind and heart a top priority.

In 2 Corinthians 11:3, Paul expressed concern that the Corinthians would fall back into the pagan culture, which held so much temptation, much like our own. We must constantly commit our thoughts to God's rule so that we can resist the deceptive temptation of the enemy. The more we study and meditate upon God's Word, the more we will recognize his voice and be able to discern it from the voice of the enemy.

We can't play around with impure thoughts. In 2 Timothy 2:22, we are told that we must *run* from them, because they will quickly lead to the greater sin of lust. As we run from impure thoughts, we can pursue faith, love, and peace instead. Surrounding ourselves with other Christians who also pursue purity will help us stand strong in the battlefield of our minds.

We are to live in the world but not be like it, because the world is impure (Titus 1:15). We are all called to serve as lights in the darkness, and we must go into the world to do that. But we must balance our time with the world against our time with God and other believers, which will strengthen us in the fight against impurity.

PURSUING HOLINESS

When you are a follower of Christ, God sees you as holy. Holy means to be set apart for special purposes, as well as clean and without fault. We can only enjoy this status because Jesus died for us and took the punishment for our sins.

Ginger Harrington writes, "Holiness is an open hand, trusting that God is sufficient for each day and every need."[3] The pursuit of holiness can be joyful if impure thoughts have plagued you for a long time. God will meet your needs in the beauty of his holiness, and he will show you the beauty of living a holy life for his glory. Meditating on holiness verses can bring you peace and life.

As believers, we have the great privilege of being living temples where the Holy Spirit takes up residence (1 Cor. 6:19–20). This is an amazing passage worth pondering. A member of the triune God resides in you—take a moment to praise him for choosing you as his child! Since Jesus paid for us with his blood, we are priceless in God's eyes, and he wants us to live a pure life in light of our calling. We can praise and thank him for choosing us by pursuing holiness with our minds and our bodies.

God chose you before the world was even created to be holy in his eyes (Eph. 1:4). Holy means to be set apart for his special use, like a gorgeous crystal vase or delicate china. God wants you to see yourself the way he sees you: special and set apart. When you begin to see yourself the way God sees you, it's easier to see how impure thoughts are cheap substitutes for the beautiful truths God longs to provide for you.

The Bible tells us in Ephesians 5:3 that we should not have even a hint of impurity as God's people—yes, that's a tall order. However, the Holy Spirit lives in you, remember? Pray directly to him when you feel tempted and ask him to ping your spirit when impure thoughts sneak in without your vigilant notice. He will help you develop the practice of guarding your heart and bouncing your eyes so that impurity becomes less and less of a problem in your life.

In 1 Peter 1:15–16, we learn that God wants us to be holy because he is holy. This is the basis for our motivation toward holiness. God calls us to be like him. We can never be completely without sin like

Jesus was, but every day, month, and year we can make progress toward a holier life. Pursuing holiness in your thought life is the main way to be conformed to Christ's holiness. In every aspect of your life, choose holiness to draw closer to God.

Because you are so special to him, don't ruin your calling with impure thoughts. Choose holiness out of a thankful and worshipful heart, and God will continually purify and renew your mind as you delight in his presence.

═══════ MORE MEDITATION VERSES ═══════

- ❧ The Lord detests the thoughts of the wicked, but gracious words are pure in his sight. (Prov. 15:26)

- ❧ One who loves a pure heart and who speaks with grace will have the king for a friend. (Prov. 22:11)

- ❧ But now he has reconciled you by Christ's physical body through death to present you holy in his sight, without blemish and free from accusation. (Col. 1:22)

- ❧ For God did not call us to be impure, but to live a holy life. (1 Thess. 4:7).

- ❧ Do not share in the sins of others. Keep yourself pure. (1 Tim. 5:22b)

- ❧ He has saved us and called us to a holy life—not because of anything we have done but because of his own purpose and grace. This grace was given us in Christ Jesus before the beginning of time. (2 Tim. 1:9)

- ❧ God the Father knew you and chose you long ago, and his Spirit has made you holy. As a result, you have obeyed him and have been cleansed by the blood of Jesus Christ. May God give you more and more grace and peace. (1 Pet. 1:2 NLT)

Prayer

Father in heaven,

I praise you for your holiness. There is no impurity in you. No sin or temptation whatsoever. Because you are holy, I can worship you with my whole heart and stand in awe of your majesty. Your perfection brings me to my knees.

I confess that I have entertained sinful thoughts that intro-duced impurity into my thought life, heart and soul. It's shameful to admit, but there are areas of struggle I've dealt with for a long time and never brought to you before. But I want that to change today, Father. Pour the cleansing blood of Jesus over my impure thoughts and reform me from the inside out. Create a new heart in me and renew my thoughts.

Thank you for dwelling in me with your Holy Spirit. Thank you for choosing me before I was born, before the world was even created. I am grateful that you call me chosen, royal, holy, and special. Help me to value myself the way you value me.

I ask you to shine a spotlight into secret impurities in my thought life, Lord. Cleanse me from them and help me resist the enemy's attack through meditation. Meet my heart's cry that lies underneath the triggers, Father. Help me choose you instead of images and rela-tionships that are poor substitutes for your abounding love.

In Jesus's name,
Amen.

REFLECTION QUESTIONS

1. What is your main trigger for impure thoughts? What will you do to eradicate it from your thought life?

2. What practical steps will you take to "flee from sexual immorality" in your thought life this week?

3. Which verse gave you new insight into the holy life God wants for you? How can you use it the next time you are tempted to entertain impure thoughts?

NOTES

[1] Stephen Arterburn, Fred Stoecker, and Mike Yorkey, *Preparing Your Son for Every Man's Battle: Honest Conversations about Sexual Integrity* (Colorado Springs: Waterbrook, 2010), 181.

[2] Donna Partow, *Becoming a Vessel God Can Use* (Minneapolis: Bethany House Publishers, 2004), 125.

[3] Ginger Harrington, *Holy in the Moment: Simple Ways to Love God and Enjoy Your Life* (Abingdon Press, 2018), Kindle version.

CHAPTER ELEVEN

PAINFUL
THOUGHTS

You keep track of all my sorrows.
You have collected all my tears in your bottle.
You have recorded each one in your book.

—PSALM 56:8 NLT

When depression settles on you, you become intimately acquainted with painful thoughts against your own will. Each one is like a paper cut inside your brain, and too many at once can cause internal bleeding.

Every painful thought I had in my dark seasons of depression was attached to the word "never." The enemy constantly planted never-bombs on the battlefield of my mind. When I entertained a painful thought, the shrapnel would fly into other areas of my soul, wounding my whole spirit.

In my childhood depressions, I had painful thoughts attached to loneliness and responsibility. Those long, lonely summers as the oldest child scraped joy from my insides like the dental assistant scrapes plaque from your teeth. I constantly worried about whether the door was locked, whether a stranger would suddenly visit, and whether my performance on chores met my mom's requirements. Loaded down with too much responsibility, unable to relax and simply be a child in a single-parent home, I believed the painful lie: *You'll never find peace.*

In my teenage depressions, my most frequent painful thoughts related to self-image. I binged on sweets and snacks to gain comfort, which packed well over fifty additional pounds on my medium-sized frame. Though I knew that every extra bite would weigh me down, I couldn't resist the soothing taste of chocolate pudding or the satisfying crunch of tortilla chips. As I stared at myself in the mirror, the painful thoughts told me: *You'll never get a date.*

Rejection from boys drove my college depressions. One semester, I enjoyed weeks of thoughtful conversation with a boy who had much in common with me, and I thought I sensed a spark. The next semester, he flatly refused to speak to me. Rejection crushed me when I drove down the mountain for work and he drove up for classes. Every time we met at the four-way stop, he was a stone who stared straight ahead. Like a vise clamping down, rejection told me: *You'll never be wanted.*

Hopelessness infected my adult depressions. Whether I dealt with marriage problems or family issues, I too often ruminated on what was going wrong. Many times when I was driving on a two-lane highway, I secretly considered veering into the oncoming traffic. The enemy flashed that idea through my mind for just a second, and then I considered my children in the back seat and the innocent driver in the other lane. Horrified, I pushed those thoughts down and didn't tell anyone. The never-thread was underneath: *Things will never change.*

Perhaps you've never dealt with depression yourself, but I guarantee you know someone who does. Painful thoughts are a hallmark of depression, a sure sign that someone is caught up in a serotonin-sapped web. I encourage you to get professional help for yourself if you are having self-destructive thoughts like the ones I described. If you notice a loved one expressing painful thoughts, don't hesitate to refer him or her to a therapist, because painful thoughts can overtake a person and cause disaster.

When I was in therapy for my depressions, I learned that pouring out your painful thoughts to God is one of the ways to let them go. The enemy uses the negative energy from each painful thought to add another brick to his destructive strongholds. By meditating on verses of healing and hope, you can retrain your mind to think positive, God-pleasing, life-giving thoughts. Depression is difficult to overcome, but God's Word holds the key to recovery.

THE STARTING POINT OF PAIN

As soon as sin entered the world, pain became a permanent problem. Eve ate the forbidden fruit and Adam accepted it from her, then shame made them hide. Pain entered Eve's most vulnerable spaces—her marriage and her motherhood (Gen. 3:16). Women have been affected by pain in those areas ever since. Our relationships are constantly challenged and worn down by pain, not only when saying "I do" or giving birth. In the same way, Adam was cursed with pain in one of his most vulnerable areas—work (Gen. 3:17). His work became tinged with toil due to sin's effects. Rather than being a joy at all times, work can be drudgery and cause us physical, emotional, and mental pain. The pain our men experience in their work or the pain we experience in our own work often flows over onto our relationships, creating a painful broken cycle.

Accepting that we live in a world cursed with pain can give you a measure of peace. I have an idealistic nature, and decades of my life passed before I learned to close the gap between my expectations and reality for greater peace. Simply realizing that pain is part of this life can help us feel less wounded. I also grew in acceptance by listening to others' stories of pain and realizing I wasn't alone in mine.

The Bible tells us to expect pain all the way up until the unknown date of Jesus's second coming. Paul writes in Romans 8:22, "We know that the whole creation has been groaning as in the pains of childbirth right up to the present time." Pain will continue to manifest itself in creation and many different areas of our lives. Accepting this truth can be the starting point of healing.

THE MANY FACETS OF PAIN

I enjoy listening to country music. It's the one music genre all five of my family members can agree on when riding in a car together. But I set limits on how often I listen to it in painful seasons. Most country songs are rooted in pain, and the more I expose myself to virtual pain, the more I am reminded of my literal pain.

Jean Lush writes, "There are certain painful emotions that will always cause us to suffer tension until we root them out of our lives. . . . Until we learn to control these emotions, we will suffer from incredible tension."[1] We must deal with our painful thoughts and emotions if we want to experience healing.

We tend to ruminate on our painful thoughts, which increases our exposure to pain. Playing painful thoughts on repeat is the enemy's way of entrenching us in his strongholds. You can break out of those strongholds by meditating on verses that specifically apply to each one. Let's look at common strongholds and verses you can use for meditation when painful thoughts enter your mind.

REJECTION

Rejection is one of the most painful aspects of the human experience. I can instantly recall dozens of times I've experienced rejection, and I'm sure you can too. We may continue to experience rejection the whole time we live on this earth. Yet God will never reject you. He promises not to reject you because you are his special possession (Ps. 94:14 NLT). He offers you comfort, affirmation, and peace when you feel rejected by others.

SEPARATION

Many of us have endured temporary or permanent separations from people we loved or situations that brought us happiness. Romans 8:38–39 tells us in a wonderful list that nothing in the earthly or spiritual realms can ever separate us from God's powerful love. Use this passage as a shield against painful thoughts. When I am feeling separated from the love I seek from others, this passage brings me comfort and renews my confidence in the Lord.

LONELINESS

Loneliness is rampant in our isolated culture. Of all the hard things in life, loneliness has plagued me more often than any other. As I mentioned before, I learned to turn to God first rather than to others in the moments when I feel lonely. Meditating on verses like Psalm 25:16 helps me remember that the Lord is my constant companion, even in my loneliest moments. When you feel lonely, get in the habit of meditating as your first line of defense. God wants to comfort you in your loneliness and will reward you with the warmth of his presence.

DEPRESSION

Having endured many seasons of depression, I've learned that they can be opportunities to draw closer to God. He doesn't call my depression sin, nor does he expect me to jump right out of it. He draws me into fellowship with him when the dark clouds weigh on my soul, and I can always find healing when his Spirit is near. Psalm 43:5 NLT tells us to put our hope in God when we feel discouraged and sad. We will feel our spirits lift when we choose to praise him despite our difficult circumstances.

SADNESS

Psalm 56:8 has brought me more comfort than any other verse when I feel sad. As a highly sensitive person with a melancholy nature, I didn't always feel understood by my family or friends. They tended to discount my sad feelings because they didn't understand them. Knowing that my sorrows matter to God has helped me feel valued. He treasures my tears because my feelings always matter to him. He has the unique ability to handle my real and imagined sorrows with perfect grace. God is tracking your sorrows in beautiful little bottles and fanciful ledgers. Someday in heaven, he will reveal how he redeemed each one.

WEAKNESS

Right after spiritual attacks in my weak areas, I often feel like I won't be able to recover. But God renews my strength as I draw close to him in prayer and meditation. This passage in Isaiah holds a promise that when you feel weak, he will infuse you with his strength. You don't need to pretend to be strong on your own; his strength will lift you up. Because he never grows weary, he can provide us strength. Picture a mighty eagle flying high in the sky, powered by God's strength. That's the picture God wants you to focus your thoughts upon when you feel weak (Isa. 40:28–31).

PERSECUTION

Are you weary from being mocked, belittled, or excluded due to your faith? Count yourself blessed. Many of our Christian brothers and sisters around the world live on the edge of violence and death due to their faith. Yet we sometimes face persecution in subtler ways in the Western world, and it hurts. I have been hurt from just this kind of suffering, and you will be subject to it too as you grow in faith. Meditate on 1 Peter 5:9 when you face persecution. It can encourage you to stand strong, since you aren't alone in your pain. You will also be comforted by knowing that God will help you recover.

Suzanne Eller writes: "Regardless of its origin, the way our heart thinks creates a distinct path that often leads us, rather than being led by us. This is where we can find ourselves in a rut. The pain is subsiding, and our heart is mending, but sometimes we create or perpetuate our own pain because of the way we think."[2] Taking control of our painful thoughts through Christian meditation can pave the path toward healing and spiritual maturity.

SEEKING GOD'S COMFORT THROUGH MEDITATION

When painful thoughts cloud your mind, you need comfort right away. God's comfort will strengthen you and help you get back on your feet after being wounded. Use Christian meditation as medicine when painful thoughts affect you.

Psalm 119:50 tells us that God's promises are our main source of comfort in affliction. The comfort of God's Word isn't a fuzzy blanket. It's a fortifying strengthener for our faith, because God always keeps his promises. When you go to God's Word first in your pain, you will gain the supernatural strength you need to face another day.

Our sufferings aren't in vain. If we suffer because we are following Jesus, God will pour out his comfort on us in showers of healing (2 Cor. 1:5). Jesus knows exactly how our pain feels, as described in Isaiah 53:4. Nothing we experience is more painful than what he endured. His sufferings hold comfort for us when we feel like no one understands our pain.

David Seamands writes: "[Jesus] understands the pain of rejection, the anxiety of separation, the terror of loneliness and abandonment, the dark clouds of depression. These infirmities, these cripplings and weaknesses, He knows, He understands, He feels. He is our Wounded Healer, the One 'wounded for our transgressions,' who 'bore our iniquities and our infirmities.'"[3] Draw close to your wounded healer whenever painful thoughts affect you.

When we are struggling with painful thoughts, we have a choice: Will we let our hearts be troubled or not? John 14:1 tells us that we can focus on believing in God rather than dwelling on our troubles. In our painful moments, we can choose to shut trouble out of our hearts by believing in and meditating upon God's promises to comfort, heal, and strengthen us.

Our sufferings have a time limit—there's such joy in that knowledge! We won't suffer forever, and someday our painful thoughts will be replaced with glory beyond imagination (Rom. 8:18). We can find great hope in Revelation 21:4. This beautiful verse holds the promise of heaven, where pain will no longer touch us. When the enemy shoves a painful sword into your thought life, meditate on this verse and remember where your hope lies.

THE PROMISE OF HEALING

When you are dealing with painful thoughts, healing may seem impossible. I've doubted that healing was possible in relationships with prodigals.

I've turned to Jesus's parable in Luke 15:11–32 many times to understand the different angles of dealing with lost loved ones.

Like the father who let his younger son leave at great cost to him, I wait for prodigals to return home. I don't chase after them, but my heart is always tethered to them in love. When I think about what they are doing in their wildernesses, the thoughts become so painful that I simply block them out or they threaten to overwhelm me. I try not to worry about the toll their wild living is exacting on them. I simply stand watching the horizon for them, trusting God to reveal all the answers for healing in his perfect timing, rather than drowning in a sea of painful thoughts.

I recently endured a barrage of painful thoughts after a difficult conversation with a prodigal, and immediately afterward I got on my knees and sobbed into a pillow. The enemy told me that hope and healing would never reach my situation. He tried to dunk me in the sea of painful thoughts.

But I claimed the promises of God; he will never leave me nor forsake me (Heb. 13:5), and by his wounds I am healed (Isa. 53:5). Because I had meditated on those two verses for many years, they were at the ready when the enemy tried to defeat me in a devastating moment.

I got up, dried my tears, and called my sisters in Christ to ask for support. After drawing close to God in prayer and getting a good night's rest, I was healed from that attack. Much faster than other times when I ruminated on my problem for days before turning to God or others for help.

Healing is possible if you seek God first, friend. Consider your painful thoughts calls to action. He wants you to run to him like you would run to the first aid kit if you were bleeding. Healing verses like Isaiah 58:8 (NLT) can help you find relief in your painful moments. Let's take a closer look.

Then your salvation will come like the dawn

The previous verses in this chapter talk about serving others with a humble heart as the kind of fasting God wants from us. He wants our hearts to be focused outward, on him and on others. When we have that type of attitude, God assures us that he will save us from the source of our pain. His salvation comes as predictably as the sunrise.

and your wounds will quickly heal.

When you look to God to save you from your painful thoughts, your wounds will heal faster. Our painful thoughts tend to be recursive, circling back on themselves in a self-defeating cycle. However, we can break the painful cycle by asking God for healing. With his divine assistance, we can watch our wounds heal before our eyes.

Your godliness will lead you forward,

As you pursue godliness rather than a self-centered, self-pitying route, you will move up and out of your painful thinking. It takes courage, strength, and godly character to shed painful thoughts and choose healing. God will reward you with forward movement as you obey his laws and follow in the path he has chosen for you.

and the glory of the LORD will protect you from behind.

Isn't it comforting to know that during the healing process, you are protected on all sides? God knows that when you are healing, you need protection from further hurt. His own glorious presence will protect you in the front, sides, and back as you walk forward in godliness.

When we cry out to God for help, acknowledging him as Lord over our situation, he will bring his healing powers to our rescue (Ps. 30:2). So often we forget to call out to him first, but he has healing ready for us when he hears our cries of pain. He is ready to heal your broken heart and bind up your wounds (Ps. 147:3). When our hearts are broken, God is the only one capable of fully healing them. He cares for us so much that he lovingly wraps our wounds with his love.

In the healing process, God offers us the peace that transcends all understanding (Phil. 4:7). That peace can carry us through our pain, and it will serve as a witness to others. We can praise God during our healing process (Jer. 17:14). Even in our painful moments, we can praise God for offering healing to us. Our healing and salvation is only possible through Jesus's suffering, death, and resurrection. He is worth all our praise, in both painful and positive times.

MORE MEDITATION VERSES

- "Peace, peace, to those far and near," says the LORD. "And I will heal them." (Isa. 57:19)

- I remember, LORD, your ancient laws, and I find comfort in them. (Ps. 119:52)

- I am suffering and in pain. Rescue me, O God, by your saving power. (Ps. 69:29 NLT)

- As a mother comforts her child, so will I comfort you. (Isa. 66:13a)

- Blessed are those who mourn, for they will be comforted. (Matt. 5:4)

Prayer

Father in heaven,

I praise you as my healer. You can heal me better than any treatment from a doctor, any counsel from a therapist, or any advice from a friend. Your healing transcends medicine or bandages. It heals my heart in places no one else sees. I love the truth that perfect healing is possible with you.

I confess that I have allowed painful thoughts to repeat in my mind without turning to you for help. I allow the enemy to gain power over me when I steep myself in painful thoughts. I want to take my pain to you to receive lasting healing and peace. I believe that the best comfort, strength, and healing I can receive is only available in relationship with you.

Thank you for suffering on my behalf, Jesus. Thank you for identifying with all my hurts. Thank you that I can come to you anytime and share my full range of pain with you. Nothing is too small or too large for you to handle, and I am grateful for your strength and affirmation.

Teach me to immediately cry out to you when painful thoughts attempt to rule my mind. Help me to turn to you first rather than to any other source for the comfort I seek. Provide me full healing for my hurts. Give me the strength to face future pain and the hope of a painless eternity with you in heaven.

In Jesus's name,
Amen.

REFLECTION QUESTIONS

1. What is the source of your current painful thoughts?

2. Which verse in this chapter brought you the most comfort?

3. Where do you most need the Lord's healing in your thought life?

NOTES

[1] Jean Lush, *Women and Stress: Practical Ways to Manage Tension* (Grand Rapids: Revell, 2008), 24.

[2] Suzanne Eller, *The Mended Heart: God's Healing for Your Broken Places* (Grand Rapids: Revell, 2014), 177.

[3] David Seamands, *Healing Your Heart of Painful Emotions* (New York: Inspirational Press, 1993), 112.

CHAPTER TWELVE

DEFEATED
THOUGHTS

*No, in all these things we are more than
conquerors through him who loved us.*

—ROMANS 8:37

Allow me to give you a glimpse into the writing life as we talk about defeated thoughts. At my local writers' conference, the editor of a writing magazine said it's the only industry of which he's aware in which professionals wear rejection as a badge of honor. Every writer I know struggles with defeated thoughts and has considered giving up at one point. Yep, that's me.

Like many of you, I was passionate about my dreams even when I was young. At the age of three, I told everyone I wanted to be an artist. I still have my sketchbooks and drawings from childhood, and the dream still shines between the lines of crayons and colored pencil. Then as a seventh grader, I decided that writing could be my other career when my language arts teacher said that she really enjoyed my Thanksgiving essay. As a teen, I dreamed about writing and illustrating children's books and held high hopes my dream would come true as soon as I graduated from college.

In high school, I won awards for art and writing and rose to the top of every class. My teachers encouraged me to enter contests and apply for scholarships. I got a full-ride scholarship to the university in my home town, and I dove into eighteen credit hours per semester as a double major in English and art.

The second semester of freshman year, I took an upper-level English literature class taught by a brilliant professor. He told us to write an essay on one of the *Canterbury Tales*. I chose to write about Chanticleer and the Fox from "The Nun's Priest's Tale." The day of grading arrived, and the professor read his favorites out loud to the whole class of undergraduate and graduate students. He saved his highest praise for mine, saying it was one of the finest pieces he'd ever read in his decades of teaching. My face glowed bright red with pride as I won first place, even though I was only a freshman.

Graduation finally arrived in December 2001. But where was I? Not writing and illustrating books. I was answering phones, sorting mail, filing, and typesetting. Nothing creative or fulfilling. One of my supervisors, a wise and bold woman, graciously explained that a college degree in the arts only meant one thing to an employer: I could set a goal and finish it. So much for the sky-high dreams I entertained in my high school and college years.

The Lord led me to a season of obscurity to refine me. But in those obscure years, I struggled every day with defeated thoughts. Did I really have my head on straight or was my mind simply in the clouds? I knew God had given me my gifts, but I couldn't find the bridge between reality and my dream. In tearful prayers, I begged God not to let my dreams die. Since I sorted the mail every day, I would sneak my boss's copy of *The New Yorker* home with me on the weekend and devour the articles and illustrations. They helped keep my dreams alive.

When I began blogging in 2010, I wondered if anyone besides my mom and best friend was reading what I wrote. I gave up and started over many times, unable to deny the creative urge. But I still dreamed about seeing my name in print. I submitted manuscripts and guest posts, hearing no at least as often as yes.

When I felt defeated, God would let me bump into my ninth-grade English teacher at the grocery store, who offered precious words of encouragement. When I felt discouraged, God would lead me to read passages in the Old Testament in which master artisans used their gifts to decorate the temple. God kept affirming my gifts and my dreams, teaching me to be patient and persistent.

Even though I often felt defeated, God kept watering and pruning my dream. Essentially, the book you are reading now grew in the soil of hundreds of defeated thoughts, mixed with seeds of hope and confidence in God. He's doing the same with your dreams and desires. When we focus on confidence through meditation, we can turn those defeated thoughts into something positive.

CONFRONTING A DEFEATED MIND-SET

When we look in the Bible for an example of a person who struggled with defeated thoughts, Gideon is a good example. The Midianites were torturing the Israelites, who cried out to God for help. God chose Gideon as the judge to deliver Israel from their oppression.

The first words Gideon heard from the angel of the Lord: "The LORD is with you, mighty warrior" (Judg. 6:12). But Gideon felt nothing like a mighty warrior. He was from the weakest clan, and he was the youngest in his family—certainly not the pick of the litter, especially in days when the oldest son and the strongest clan were revered. But God proved to Gideon that he was the chosen leader through a series of miracles, and Gideon accepted the challenge.

Gideon still worked with a defeated mind-set, even though he had interacted with the angel of the Lord. He tore down his family's altar to foreign idols but did it at night because he was afraid of what people would think. Indeed, a hostile crowd gathered the next day and demanded his death. But God protected him from harm as promised, and the Holy Spirit came upon Gideon to rally troops for battle against the Midianites.

The Lord confronted Gideon's defeated mind-set head on. Gideon gathered 32,000 troops, but God cut the final number down to 300 men who would go into battle against the Midianite army. Talk about a confidence shake-up! We would all be fighting off defeated thoughts in a situation like that. Yet God wanted to prove his strength through Israel's weakness, and he chose Gideon to be his leader.

The 300 men defeated the entire Midianite army with a ridiculous combination of trumpets, empty jars, and torches. Only God could bring those elements together to produce a victory. Through Gideon's service, the Israelites enjoyed forty years of peace. Only God can transform our defeated mind-sets into blessings for many other people.

What about you? Are you facing an insurmountable challenge with the wrong tools and not enough help, like Gideon? Are you stuck in a situation that has no foreseeable ending? Are defeated thoughts keeping you from choosing God's best for your life?

Nicki Koziarz writes, "When our circumstances don't change, we only have two choices: settle and pout, or shift and praise."[1] We can either fall prey to our defeated thoughts and live a less-than life or choose to focus on the Lord God Almighty, who will work through us. As Paul wrote in 2 Corinthians 12:9, "But he said to me, 'My grace is sufficient for you, for my power is made perfect in weakness.' Therefore I will boast all the more gladly about my weaknesses, so that Christ's power may rest on me." Consider your defeated thoughts triggers to seek God's strength instead of your own, so that he gets all the glory for accomplishing something great through you.

The enemy will attempt to keep you in a defeated mind-set so that God's glory is subdued. It's his plan to hold you back with doubt, because he doesn't want you to reach your full potential for service in God's kingdom. Charles Stanley writes, "If [Satan] notices you turning a fearful or insecure ear to listen to his accusations, he will open up a full assault on your emotions until you have collapsed in the dust of disappointment."[2] You must tune your ears to what God's voice sounds like through meditation and prayer, so that you will recognize the sneaky whispers of defeat that the enemy tries to get you to believe.

HANDLING DEFEATED THOUGHTS THROUGH MEDITATION

We unknowingly set ourselves up for failure through defeated thinking. When is the last time you thought, "I can't do this," so you don't even try? For example, most of us can relate to the struggle with weight loss. It's so easy to defeat ourselves in our thought lives before we ever take a bite of salad instead of pizza or step on a treadmill. Without calling on the Holy Spirit for help, we often feel defeated before we even begin our greatest challenges.

You'll see all kinds of memes on social media to stir your self-motivation. But even the prettiest or smartest meme doesn't have the living power of God's Word. Be careful with any phrase or statement or plaque that proclaims the power of self. Inspirational quotes can be useful for motivation, but for total thought-life transformation, Scripture has no match.

Defeated thoughts lead to a downcast spirit. But God will lift up anyone who feels downcast if they seek his rescue (Job 22:29). If you are feeling downcast by defeated thoughts, pour your heart out to God and ask him to lift you out of your low places. He will answer your heartfelt prayer.

Defeated thoughts can make us feel like we are drowning. Psalm 18:16–19 uses the metaphor of deep waters for our defeated thoughts. If others caused or were involved in our defeat, we can feel weighed down by shame and sorrow. Because God is strong and powerful and mighty to save, he can pull us out of our deepest defeats and set us in a new place of growth. He delights in you and loves to defend you in front of your physical and spiritual enemies.

No matter who stands against you, they cannot stand against God (Rom. 8:31). I've found comfort in this verse when facing legal battles, persecution, church struggles, and family problems. When you feel like everyone is opposing you, meditate on Romans 8:31–37. It will give you much-needed strength. No hard thing can remove us from the reach of God's love, which is always nearby. We can call ourselves conquerors because God empowers us with his abundant love.

PURSUING CONFIDENCE IN CHRIST

My daughter, the baby of our family, was born with confidence. She has no trouble saying the word "no," unlike her mom. I'm sure it's partly due to her God-given personality. Maybe it's because she grew up in a two-parent home and felt more secure than I did. Maybe it's because she's the youngest child with two older brothers, while I was the oldest of sisters. I've heard from women in similar situations that their older brothers always protected them.

When I was young, I secretly wished for an older brother who would go first and take on the responsibility. I was born a leader, but I didn't always want to be one. I struggled with confidence even into my adult years. Passivity and I had a toxic relationship for decades, which often set me up for defeat. Until my relationships suffered enough, I didn't learn that my being passive was costing me God's best.

I've learned that I had an "older brother" all along. Jesus was leading the way for me. His strength and power are more than enough for both of us. I had to trust in the confidence Jesus provided me, rather than focusing on my own weaknesses, to start living a confident and assertive life. This took practice and many small defeats before I was courageous enough to live the life God calls me to live.

Maybe you struggle with confidence as well; most of us women have struggled in this area at one time or another. You can turn to Jesus to lead the way in your pursuit of confidence. You can ask him to give you confidence in what he can do through you. Confidence in Jesus is available no matter how defeated you feel. He is willing and able to take your fears, doubts, frustrations, and weaknesses and transform them into a glorious victory through his strength and power.

When you are seeking confidence, Christian meditation can empower your mind-set. It can destroy the doubts and fears that the enemy places in your thought life. Let's look at verses from Psalm 27 to find confidence in God:

> The LORD is my light and my salvation—
> whom shall I fear?
> The LORD is the stronghold of my life—
> of whom shall I be afraid? (v. 1)

I have printed this verse on a pretty background and placed it near my makeup counter. When I am "putting my face on" every morning, I glance over at it and meditate upon it. This verse helps shield me from defeated thoughts because I sense God's strength protecting me in it. He is my light for dark valleys and my salvation when I need to be rescued. Like a high, strong tower, he is my fear-fighting stronghold. When I put on this armor every morning through meditation, I feel like a conqueror in Jesus with nothing to fear from the enemy.

> *Though an army besiege me,*
> *my heart will not fear;*
> *though war break out against me,*
> *even then I will be confident. (v. 3)*

We may not face literal armies every day like David did. However, we all have battles to face in our relationships and life circumstances. When you feel like you are caught up in relational, situational, or spiritual warfare, this verse will give you the confidence you need to face them. Remember the truths in verse 1—they will help you remember who is on your side when you face tough battles. Since Jesus is your Savior, you need not fear that the attacks will destroy you.

> *For in the day of trouble*
> *he will keep me safe in his dwelling;*
> *he will hide me in the shelter of his sacred tent*
> *and set me high upon a rock. (v. 5)*

You can have confidence even on your worst days because God is protecting you. I love the word pictures in this encouraging verse. God draws you into his own house to protect you. He hides you from the enemy and sets you in the sacred space of his powerful presence. When the storms rage, he hides you in the cleft of a rock, where no harm can reach your soul. Take comfort knowing that God builds your confidence through his protection.

Then my head will be exalted
above the enemies who surround me;
at his sacred tent I will sacrifice with shouts of joy;
I will sing and make music to the LORD (v. 6)

What is our response to all this wonderful knowledge? Praise God! As you meditate on the verses of Psalm 27, let praises rise in your heart. Shout in confidence and joy; sing a personal song of thanksgiving to him. Whether you can carry a tune or not, God adores the music you offer in praise just for his hearing. He will lift up your head over your enemies—let this truth strengthen your confidence in him.

Look for God's goodness every day, and your confidence in him will grow. As you watch the Lord destroying your defeated thoughts and uplifting others, thank and praise him for his goodness (Ps. 27:13). He always makes good on his promises, and tracking the victories will strengthen your faith.

God promises to give us peace and a calm, secure confidence when we live a righteous life. Righteousness is living a life of wise choices that are obedient to God's laws. To overcome your defeated thoughts, repent of all wrongdoing and make necessary changes. Greater confidence is waiting for you if you prioritize righteousness (Isa. 32:17).

If you struggle with praying in confidence, remember that Jesus has thrown open the doors to heaven's throne through his death and resurrection. You can enter his presence directly through prayer and meditation (Eph. 3:12). Our faith gives us confidence in what we do not see but believe in our hearts, as noted in Hebrews 11:1. The more your faith grows, the more hope and assurance you will have in the fulfillment of God's promises. Faith and confidence in Christ grow parallel to one another.

It's common to feel defeated, because your journey isn't yet finished. Keep your eyes fixed on the promise-filled future rather than the struggles of the present. Meditating on Philippians 1:6 can help you focus on the hopeful future. Your confidence rests in God's completion of your good works, not in you figuring it all out right now.

MORE MEDITATION VERSES

❧ For you have been my hope, Sovereign LORD, my confidence since my youth. (Ps. 71:5)

❧ But blessed is the one who trusts in the LORD, whose confidence is in him. (Jer. 17:7)

❧ Such confidence we have through Christ before God. (2 Cor. 3:4)

❧ And now, dear children, continue in him, so that when he appears we may be confident and unashamed before him at his coming. (1 John 2:28)

Prayer

Father in heaven,

I praise you as the strength of my heart. No one is more power-ful than you. No one shares your glory or creative ability or power to save. You are transcendent over all things, including the struggles in my life. Your omnipotence inspires me to worship you.

I confess that defeated thoughts often become roadblocks in my walk of faith. I fall prey to the fears, doubts, and insecurities they release in my mind. Because I get stuck in defeated thinking, I don't always choose your best path for my life, and my service to you and others is a fraction of what it could be.

Thank you for giving me your confidence, Jesus. I don't have to generate it on my own; I can simply trust you to provide it for me. Thank you that your strength, power, and might can be mine in difficult situations. Thank you for giving me the opportunity to display your glory through my weaknesses.

Holy Spirit, I pray that you would help me identify defeated thoughts as soon as they enter my mind. Help me turn them into faith-building bricks rather than the dust of further disappointment. I want my faith to grow; help me gain confidence in you so I can live the best life possible for your renown.

In Jesus's name,
Amen.

REFLECTION QUESTIONS

1. When have defeated thoughts threatened to derail your path of service to God?

2. What is your main takeaway from Gideon's story?

3. Which verse inspired new confidence for you?

NOTES

[1]Nicki Koziarz, *Why Her?: 6 Truths We Need to Hear When Measuring Up Leaves Us Falling Behind* (B&H Publishing Group, 2018), Kindle edition.

[2]Charles F. Stanley, *Landmines in the Path of the Believer: Avoiding the Hidden Dangers* (Nashville: Thomas Nelson, 2007), 82.

CHAPTER THIRTEEN

REGRETFUL THOUGHTS

Godly sorrow brings repentance that leads to salvation and leaves no regret, but worldly sorrow brings death.

—2 CORINTHIANS 7:10

When I was a teen, I learned the art of holding a boy at arm's length. I knew a certain boy liked me, and I wouldn't admit to myself that I liked him. Still, we danced circles around one another, charting each other's social moves with detailed secret maps.

After a disastrous ending to another relationship (culminating at prom—how appropriate for teen drama, right?), I was D.O.N.E. with boys. Unfortunately, Arm's Length Boy assumed that since I had broken up with Prom Boy, I was available. After a protracted wait, he made his first real move.

I was sitting in my desk at the front of the classroom, reading a paperback copy of *Jurassic Park* before class began. He stopped by my desk and asked me if the book was any good. Now, I'm one of the world's biggest book lovers—I read more than one hundred titles a year. It's the perfect inroad question for someone like me. But because I had been wounded by another boy less than a week before, I grouped all boys into one negative category: Completely Untrustworthy. Including this boy.

I looked up into Arm's Length Boy's face and spoke a curt "Yep." My tone was clear—*I don't want to talk to you.* He lingered for another moment as I tried to dive back into the dinosaur world. Then he headed to his desk at the back of the room.

The longest fifty minutes of my life unfolded next. Regret crashed over me like waves, sweeping me in its undertow. The pounding waves kept me from thinking about anything except how horribly I had treated an innocent victim. What could I do to make this right? Passing him a note was too risky; crying out in class would have been social suicide. As I weighed my options, the bell rang.

He walked out in a huff. I tracked his head as he got swept up in the throng of peers descending the steps. A desperate cry surged up inside me. Five years of dancing around the truth propelled this cry. At the top of the steps, I almost shouted his name. But a dark inner voice whispered to my soul: *Who really wants you anyway?* I was silenced.

In 2010 I had been married for ten years and had three children. Memories of Arm's Length Boy kept surfacing for the first time in many years, unbidden. I asked God what to do with them, and he said, "Write." While my children were napping, I wrestled with shame while I typed out every memory I had of him. I filled page after page with tears and heartache, linked to other family hurts and losses.

Writing about Arm's Length Boy led me to seek counseling. It also led me to start blogging. A lot of good came out of writing those memories. But regret was my constant companion. I couldn't shake it, no matter how hard I prayed, how much I wrote, or how many times I told the stories to my friends or my therapist.

In 2012, my grandpa died, and my church sent me booklets on grief every six weeks. Every time I read one of those booklets, Arm's Length Boy's face flashed in my mind. I got irritated with myself; wasn't I supposed to be grieving my dear grandpa rather than this boy I hadn't seen in decades? Still, God pressed me to mourn this relationship that had never materialized and didn't end well. Only through months of grief did I finally put my regret to rest.

I learned an important life lesson that doesn't often show up in movies or novels: Sometimes you don't get another chance. Sometimes you must accept the mess you made and move forward. Though I can't go back and make that situation right, I am hoping God will set everything right in the end. I am no longer chained to a past littered with regret. I'm clinging to hope only God can promise.

THE BURDEN OF REGRET

Regret can make forward movement impossible. When you pair it with guilt and shame, it can feel like a five-hundred-pound pallet of bricks you must drag behind you every day. Nothing is more effective at putting the brakes on your faith journey than regret. We feel regret over what we have done or what we haven't done. Both types of regret can render us ineffective for God's purposes. Let's look at both types in detail.

Some of our regrets are sins of commission, meaning that we actively cause damage to our relationship with God, ourselves, and others. Sins of commission are when we're willfully disobedient.

You willfully disobey God when you act like Jonah, heading west when God tells you to head east. You willfully sin against yourself with self-harm or gluttony. You willfully sin against others by using your actions or words to hurt them. It's relatively easy to notice the effects of sins of commission, because they are overt.

Sins of omission are less obvious, yet they are just as destructive. They are knowing the right thing to do but refusing to do it, usually for selfish or self-protective reasons. My teenage incident with Arm's Length Boy is a sin of omission. I've committed other sins of omission by not giving due to stinginess, not apologizing out of stubbornness, and choosing to keep reading instead of spending quality time with my children. Sins of omission withhold blessings. They squeeze relationships dry through neglect. While sins of commission destroy with fire, sins of omission destroy with ice.

I'm thankful for Paul's honest account of both types of sin in Romans 7. I'll list his points in single lines for our meditation:

> *For I do not understand my own actions.*
> *For I do not do what I want,*
> *but I do the very thing I hate.*
> *For I have the desire to do what is right,*
> *but not the ability to carry it out.*
> *For I do not do the good I want,*
> *but the evil I do not want is what I keep doing.*
> *(Rom. 7:15, 18a–19 ESV)*

Can you identify with Paul's struggle with both the sins of omission and the sins of commission, even at the same time? He shows us that we aren't alone in our regret for the wrong things we've done.

If anyone in history was ever tempted with regret, it had to be Paul, who approved the murder of Christians before he became one himself. I can't imagine how regret must have haunted his thought life every day after he was saved.

In Romans 7:24–25 ESV, Paul comes to the end of himself and finds his solution:

> *Wretched man that I am!*
> *Who will deliver me from this body of death?*
> *Thanks be to God through Jesus Christ our Lord!*

Do you also feel wretched at the end of your regret rope? Do you want to lay down that rope that forces you to drag a pallet of bricks behind you? There is hope for you in Jesus, who will deliver you from your past. Christian meditation can pave the way to that hope.

THE IMPORTANCE OF GRIEF

I once heard a sermon by Adrian Rogers that described grief as a love word. You can't grieve something you didn't care about. Regret is also tied to love. Until we let go of regret through grief, we can't fully reconnect with Love himself and the hope he promises.

You've probably heard about the five stages of grief. They are denial, anger, bargaining, depression, and acceptance. These steps often don't flow in organized fashion. They bubble up in different order over time. But you must wade through them all to reach acceptance, and God can help you reach the shoreline in perfect peace.

Our theme verse for this chapter points to grief. Let's look at it in pieces:

> *Godly sorrow brings repentance*

Regret is tied to a sin, as we discussed. Grieving that sin can bring health and healing to our hearts. Worthy sorrow is from God and turns us toward truth, grace, and life, away from our sin.

that leads to salvation and leaves no regret,

When we set our past sins free through grieving what never was or what can never be made right, we choose salvation. We choose to be covered with the blood of Jesus's sacrifice, which cleanses us from our sins of commission and omission. Jesus alone can set us free from the burdens of regret.

but worldly sorrow brings death.

Simply feeling sorry for something you did or didn't do doesn't bring health and life. You must accept that Jesus covers your sins with his sacrifice, or you risk being condemned for those past sins. Repentance is part of the grieving process. You can't rewrite the past, but you can move forward in a God-pleasing path, refusing to repeat the same sins. Otherwise, you are choosing destruction.

Martyn Lloyd-Jones wrote, "It is always wrong to mortgage the present by the past, it is always wrong to allow the past to act as a brake upon the present."[1] We must learn to let go of our past sins to choose the best life God has waiting for us in the present.

HANDLING REGRET THROUGH MEDITATION

The Bible provides several key verses for dealing with regret. We can find freedom in these verses when regret threatens to weigh us down.

Isaiah 1:18 is a helpful verse for dealing with sins of commission. No matter how serious the sin you committed, Jesus freely offers you forgiveness and release. He will completely cleanse you from the sin, so it no longer has power over you. He's willing to settle with you; simply come to Jesus with your confession and repentance, and the deal is done. He will make your mind and heart as white as snow, pure and free from regret.

I like to apply Luke 9:23 to my sins of omission. Jesus tells us that we must take up our crosses daily, deny ourselves, and follow him. Some matters can't be fixed, but their effects can be felt for years. They can be crosses that we bear from choices we should have made. I think of their consequences as part of the responsibility God asks me to bear. We deny ourselves by refusing to get dragged down in guilt and shame. Jesus will help us bear our burdens as we follow him, and they won't feel as heavy anymore (see Matt. 11:28–30).

Staying stuck in regret is a form of childish thinking, as described in 1 Corinthians 13:11. A mature Christian doesn't dwell on the past. She takes responsibility for her actions and moves forward in God's grace. God doesn't want any of us to stay stuck in one mind-set for the rest of our lives. There is an appointed time for us to repent from our sins and grieve what was lost. Then God calls us to keep growing and maturing, and we must put regretful thoughts behind us to move forward.

The apostle Paul is such an inspiring person, especially when it comes to the topic of regret. He actively persecuted Christians before he came to faith. Though no other human being in history has done more to spread the gospel, he still considered himself unfinished. He chose to forget the sins of his past and press forward with the greater purpose God called him to pursue. He intentionally left his condemning past behind to pursue the heavenly goals God gave him (Phil. 3:12–14). His testimony can inspire us to do the same. God wants you to release your grip on the past, so you can push forward to a brighter tomorrow, full of hope and life.

HEALING THROUGH HOPE

When we have a relationship with Jesus, we have the ultimate hope of heaven. That's where regret will no longer burden us. We will even have the chance to make amends in heaven, in new ways that don't involve awkward encounters or painful recollections.

This is my hope for the redemption of my messy teenage story. I know Arm's Length Boy was a follower of Jesus, and I believe we will see each other in heaven someday. I'm picturing a bright, beautiful field that God is reserving for us. One afternoon in heaven, we will walk beside each other where no more barriers exist. Where regret, sorrow, and hurt can't touch us. The past won't have power over us any longer. We will talk like a brother and sister and work it out in complete understanding. We will rejoice in the shared love of our Savior, who is making all things new (Rev. 21:5).

Friend, God has fields of hope prepared for you too. If you can meet on an earthly field now and make things right this side of heaven, don't wait. Pray about it first and seek wise counsel, then walk that field with the person you hurt and do what you can to show them you have repented. If that's not possible or wise, place your hope in God. He knows all the regrets of your heart and will either wash them away or repair them in the heavenly places.

Every time you are tempted to dwell on regretful thoughts, the enemy binds you to the past. But God wants you to focus on the bright, beautiful future that awaits you as a believer. Through Christian meditation, you can reset your mind on hope when regretful thoughts plague you.

Jeremiah 29:11 is a popular verse because we all need greater hope and the promise of a bright future. Reorienting our focus on verses that are future-focused can lift our thoughts out of the past. This verse shows you that God is on your side as you work to put the past behind you. He has master plans that will move you forward, out of your regrets and into hope-filled purposes.

God doesn't say we should never look back. We can learn much about ourselves and our faith walk by looking back from time to time. Lamentations 3:19–23 tells us that Jeremiah looked back on times that caused regret and sorrow. However, as Christians our thoughts should be forward-focused and hope-filled. By focusing on God's love, compassion, and faithfulness, we resist the enemy's backward pull in our thought lives.

I'm sure you've put your hope in something or someone that eventually disappointed you, like I have. But our hope in God never disappoints us (Rom. 5:5 NLT). He seals hope in our hearts with the Holy Spirit's presence when we believe. God's great love is the fulfillment of our hope, and he will never let us down.

The scriptures are our main source of hope (Rom. 15:4). They teach us God's truth, provide us with the power to endure through trials, and give us encouragement for moving forward. Study and meditate on them daily to keep your mind fixed on the future where hope resides. You'll find no hope in past regrets, but you will find hope in the promises of God for both the present and the future.

> *This hope is a strong and trustworthy anchor for our souls.*
> *It leads us through the curtain into God's inner sanctuary.*
> *Jesus has already gone in there for us.*
> *(Heb. 6:19–20a NLT)*

Hope is an anchor in your mind, heart, and soul. By focusing on hope, we can have strength in all our difficulties. Our hope helps us develop a close relationship with God, where we find perfect relief from our regrets. Choose hope to gain even more access to Jesus in your daily faith walk. He is waiting for you in the inner sanctuary of heaven, where regret can no longer touch you.

MORE MEDITATION VERSES

> ↝ Forget the former things; do not dwell on the past.
> (Isa. 43:18)

❧ The LORD is good to those whose hope is in him, to the one who seeks him. (Lam. 3:25)

❧ But as for me, I watch in hope for the LORD, I wait for God my Savior; my God will hear me. (Mic. 7:7)

❧ Be joyful in hope, patient in affliction, faithful in prayer. (Rom. 12:12)

❧ For through the Spirit, by faith, we ourselves eagerly wait for the hope of righteousness. (Gal. 5:5 ESV)

❧ May our Lord Jesus Christ himself and God our Father, who loved us and by his grace gave us eternal encouragement and good hope, encourage your hearts and strengthen you in every good deed and word. (2 Thess. 2:16–17)

❧ Put all your hope in the gracious salvation that will come to you when Jesus Christ is revealed to the world. (1 Pet. 1:13b NLT)

Prayer

Father in heaven,

I praise you as my source of hope. Because you have set me free from sin's bondage, I have the promise of a pain-free future where my past will no longer have power over me. You are worthy of all the praise I can offer.

I confess that I have entertained regretful thoughts when you wanted me to let them go. I have obsessed over the things I have done wrong and the things I have left undone. But there's no going back and redoing them now. I can only trust that you will help me make things right, either in the present or in heaven someday. I am sorry I committed the sins that caused pain to myself and others.

Thank you for forgiving my sins, Lord. The sins I know I've done and the sins I have yet to realize. I thank you for taking my place on the cross for my sins of commission and omission. I need your coverage for all of them, Jesus.

Help me choose hope rather than dwelling on the past. I don't want to be stuck there anymore. I want to move forward into the bright future you have promised for me. Remind me that the past no longer has power over me since you have set me free. Inspire new hope in me every time I meditate on your Word.

In Jesus's name,
Amen.

REFLECTION QUESTIONS

1. What is your deepest regret over a sin of commission?

2. What sin of omission has caused you to regret the past?

3. How can hope in the future God promises you bring healing to both of those sins?

NOTE

[1] D. Martyn Lloyd-Jones, *Spiritual Depression: Its Causes and Its Cure* (Grand Rapids: Eerdmans Printing Company, 1992), 83.

CHAPTER FOURTEEN

ANGRY THOUGHTS

"In your anger do not sin": Do not let the sun go down while you are still angry.

—EPHESIANS 4:26

I f you love an addict or an abuser, anger deeply affects you. In my story, alcohol stands at the doorway of every single one of my deepest heartaches, and on the other side of the door, an inferno of anger steadily burns.

Like many of you, I did not grow up in a home where anger was properly handled. In my home, anger was either buried underground or subversively delivered with passive aggression. Years of repressed anger led to my depressions, because my body and spirit could no longer contain the cauldron of poisonous anger.

Add a thousand incidents of alcohol abuse on top of that, and you have a ticking time bomb set to burst on an undisclosed date.

Add a spouse who grew up in a home where anger was handled through explosions, and you have a gal with a completely wrecked thought life when it comes to angry thoughts.

A few years ago, after an argument with a loved one, God gave me a picture of the anger hidden in my heart. I have a collection of journals, which have a simple red or black leatherlike cover with crosshatched paper inside. In my conversation with God as I unburdened myself, he showed me a glimpse of thousands and thousands of those journals, stacked up high into walls and laid out lengthwise like paving bricks.

He said that each one of my secret, stuffed-down incidents of anger was like a journal filled to the brim with hatred and malice. To get free from anger's choke hold, I had to practice self-control and figuratively throw each one of those journals into a purifying fire, where God would bring beauty from ashes. He showed me green branches in that same vision, telling me that new life is possible once I surrender my anger to him.

Ironically, God is calling me to keep an anger journal right now. I simply write in it to record how alcohol's effects on my loved ones have made me boil with internal anger in hundreds of different ways. When the pen touches the page, the rage flows out in black ink. But then it's out, and I feel freer each time I complete an entry. Anger no longer chokes us when we find a healthy way to release it.

I am not intentionally keeping a record of wrongs, which is the opposite of love as described in 1 Corinthians 13. By writing my angry thoughts, I am processing my anger in a safe space, releasing it through the controlled, private boundaries of a pen's narrow path. I will someday burn it in a purifying fire, even though I've carefully preserved and kept the dozens of other journals I've written. This anger journal is a special, necessary, and temporary journal for my healing. Maybe you need to start keeping an anger journal too.

Anger is like fire: it can do good when controlled, but it can wreak havoc when unmonitored or wildly released. Self-control is the key to handling anger in God-pleasing ways. In the heat of an angry moment, Christian meditation can help you discharge your anger even better than counting to ten or taking deep breaths. Let's explore what the Bible has to say about anger and how we can control it through meditation.

DIFFERENT FORMS OF ANGER

Anger can be handled in several unhealthy ways. It can explode, it can be shared covertly through passive aggression, or it can be internalized. These methods do not solve the underlying problems and usually cause greater harm than the original anger trigger. If we don't deal with anger, it can develop into bitterness, which eats away our souls and harms our relationship with God and others.

Christian counselor and radio host June Hunt has identified four sources of anger: hurt, fear, frustration, and injustice.[1] When you notice angry thoughts on the battleground of your mind, capture them and identify their source. If you can parse them out into one of these four areas, you can deal with the underlying emotion and stop anger in its tracks. Each of these four sources of anger shows up in the Bible, and we can learn much from the examples God recorded for us in his Word.

For an example of hurt-based anger, we can look at Esau. Esau was the firstborn son of Isaac and Rebekah. He carelessly gave up his birthright to his twin brother Jacob. Jacob followed his mother's instructions and tricked his father into bestowing the blessing on him instead of Esau. When Esau discovered that Jacob had stolen the birthright, he cried out in pain (Gen. 27:34).

Esau had a right to be angry, even though he had created the situation. He was hurt because he had lost something he could never regain. He probably felt hurt that his brother turned on him. However, Esau apparently did not take his hurt to God. His hurt quickly turned into rage, which led him to want to destroy Jacob. His hurt, anger, and rage caused even more family division than was already present.

The Bible also records a clear example of fear as the source of anger. God had appointed Saul as the first king of Israel, but Saul was not a man after God's own heart like David. Through a series of willfully disobedient acts, Saul lost God's favor. David, however, gained favor with both God and the Israelites through his displays of faith and valor. As David became more successful, Saul became fearful of losing power. When David returned from battle, the Israelite women sang and danced, saying that Saul had killed thousands, but David had killed tens of thousands of enemies.

Saul couldn't stand this comparison. His anger is recorded in 1 Samuel 18:8. He was indignant that anyone besides him should be lauded, and he began viewing David with suspicion. The Lord allowed Saul to be influenced by an evil spirit, and he threw a spear at David while he was playing a harp to bring peace to Saul's household. After David dodged the spear two times, Saul was afraid (1 Sam. 18:12). He knew that God was no longer with him but had chosen David instead. His fear-based anger caused him to chase David for years, hoping to kill him.

To understand anger with frustration at its core, we can look at the story of Cain and Abel. God had apparently asked for animal sacrifices as the right form of worship. Cain was a crops farmer; Abel was a cattle farmer. Cain chose to bring his crops as an offering, and Abel brought choice portions from his firstborn flocks. God accepted Abel's sacrifice but did not accept Cain's sacrifice.

The Bible records that Cain was very angry due to God's choice (Gen. 4:5). We can infer that he felt frustrated since his gift was not "good enough." However, we can also infer that based on what God said to Cain in Genesis 4:7, Cain knew God's preference. God knew that sin was ready to pounce on Cain if he didn't sort out his frustration. Instead of taking responsibility for his unwillingness to accept God's rules, Cain took revenge on Abel, committing the first murder. Cain was eventually driven from the garden, outside of God's presence, because he didn't handle his anger in an appropriate way.

When we are angry due to injustice, we are most like God, because he is perfectly just. Jacob had worked for Laban for years, even though Laban had tricked him many times. Jacob met every requirement when he decided to go out on his own. Yet Laban pursued him as if Jacob had not fulfilled his obligations. Jacob got angry and rebuked Laban, bringing up the injustice (Gen. 31:36–42). Laban finally relented and made a covenant of peace with Jacob.

Our anger can either lead to a murderous desire or a peaceful solution. When we learn to identify the source, we can direct our anger in a healthier direction. If we refuse to take control of our anger, it will threaten to dominate us.

GOD'S ANGER

Anger itself is not wrong or sinful. God showed his anger in many different instances, and since God is holy, anger cannot be wrong when handled correctly.

Have you ever exploded in anger? Has anyone ever exploded in anger at you? No matter how angry we feel, our anger can't compare with God's anger. He is the only one who has the right to explode (Ps. 76:7 NLT), and when the final judgment comes someday, we will see it in its spectacular glory.

God is angriest when we disobey him and refuse to appreciate the relationship he offers. He was angry at the ancient Israelites for this sin. In his righteous anger, he forced them to wander in the wilderness for forty years before they received the Promised Land (Ps. 95:10). He gets angry at people today for forsaking relationship with him. When we turn our hearts away from him and refuse to obey, we arouse God's anger.

Yet God's anger is not his dominant characteristic. Because God loves us so much, he doesn't stay angry with us. If we are his followers, he shows us mercy and love instead of wrath. He loves to pardon our sins and forgive us our trespasses, because we are his chosen people (Mic. 7:18).

Jesus was angry with the Pharisees for their hard hearts, full of judgment and disbelief. Though Jesus had no sin in him, the Pharisees continued to look for ways to catch him in a mistake, so they could incriminate him (Mark 3:4–6). His anger toward their unreasonable actions was warranted. We must constantly ask God to show us any Pharisee-like thoughts in our minds so we can remove them before they multiply.

Jesus also got angry at people who were exchanging money in the temple courts (John 2:13–16). When we begin thinking that Jesus only showed love, we need to meditate on this passage. His righteous anger drove him to decisive action. Jesus is not passive; he actively controls when and how he shows his anger. We can look to Jesus for examples of how to handle our injustice-based anger.

HANDLING ANGER THROUGH MEDITATION

Over time, key Bible verses have helped me manage my anger in God-pleasing ways. I now know to go to God first when I feel angry, because my angry feelings don't stir up any sin in him. He can help me sort them out better than anyone else.

I've also learned to pick the right times to confront others. The best time to talk about my angry feelings is not after a long day when everyone is tired, no matter how justified I feel. Sometimes I pray and journal late into the night before confronting the next morning with a clearer head. Other times, prayer and journaling teach me to let my anger go and work it out with God alone rather than getting involved in a confrontation that won't produce any changes.

You'll need to pray over these verses and ask God to show you how to apply them when angry thoughts take over your mind. He may lead you to apply them differently in various situations. A close dependence upon God is key to managing your angry thoughts.

Remember that anger is *always* a call to action. Sometimes the action is simply prayer. Other times you must confront. Don't let it simmer inside. Don't let it leak out in passive aggression. Don't let it explode. Ask yourself what feeling lies underneath your anger and deal with that first. Then proceed where God leads you.

Ephesians 4:26–27 is a good meditation verse when you need help handling your anger.

"In your anger do not sin"

I find great relief in this passage. Here, God shows us that anger itself is not sinful. We don't need to beat ourselves up for getting angry. However, we must practice self-control by refusing to sin when we are angry. This requires much prayer, practice, and meditation the very moment anger rises up.

Do not let the sun go down while you are still angry,

This passage contains a principle on timing, not a literal directive. It means to keep short accounts with God and others when you are angry. A twenty-four-hour rule is useful if the anger flares up at night. I have learned through experience that most problems are handled better in the light of day. However, if you sense God prompting you to handle the matter before going to bed, exercise self-control and restraint while having your discussion.

and do not give the devil a foothold.

Failing to keep short accounts allows the enemy to have a field day in your thought life, so be sure to deal with your anger as quickly as possible. The longer you put it off, the more time the enemy has to build a stronghold of bitterness and resentment in your heart. When I apply this verse to my longest-held grudges, I can see that my lack of dealing with anger opened opportunity for the enemy. I'm still learning to submit these footholds to God and let him handle my hurt, fear, frustration, and injustice.

Proverbs 22:24–25 proves that your angry reactions are directly affected by those in your sphere of influence. That's why our families of origin have such power over our angry reactions today. You can choose now to sort through your anger influences from the past and refuse to form close relationships with those who don't handle anger in God-pleasing ways. If you are surrounded by angry people, you are probably angrier than necessary due to their negative influence, and you need to consider switching your social circles. If you choose to stay in a relationship with an angry person, you can draw close to God so you aren't tempted to fight fire with fire.

James 1:19–20 tells us to be slow to become angry, because our anger does not produce the life God wants for us. Since God is slow to anger, we must attempt to be slow to anger ourselves. Julie Clinton writes: "How often do we get mad at other people on the road when the real problem is our own irresponsibility and tardiness? Think about how often we get angry with someone who obstructs our path, whether we are looking for the quickest checkout line at the grocery store or the quickest way to advance in our careers."[2] It's wise to take a daily inventory of anger to determine whether it is valid or self-centered. Some of us are quick to anger every day! God can help us control our anger, which will help us live more peacefully with him and with others.

PURSUING SELF-CONTROL

Of all the fruits of the Spirit listed in Galatians 5:22–23, the fruit of self-control is often the hardest one for me to bear, particularly when it comes to anger. I will always be tempted to hypercontrol my anger through analysis ad nauseam, rather than risking confrontation. You may be tempted to let your anger explode without first thinking through the consequences. We all need the Holy Spirit to bear extra self-control in our lives when we are angry, wherever we fall on the expression spectrum.

You can catch angry thoughts in a self-control net, so you learn to respond rather than react in a heated moment. Meditate on self-control verses and memorize them to have them ready the next time your temper flares.

Our lips get us into much trouble when we are angry. Who hasn't spewed out unloving or harsh words in anger? But God is ready to serve as a guard over our lips (Ps. 141:3). This short, memorable verse can serve as a shield over your mouth as soon as anger rises in you. It also reminds you that God is willing to control and guard what you say when you allow his reign over your life.

Angry thoughts will enter our minds when we are provoked. However, we can choose whether to let them enter our hearts. We must guard our hearts, because they determine whether our paths ahead will be filled with strife or peace (Prov. 4:23). Through self-control, we can capture the thoughts and examine them with God's help, then deal with the root problem in a calm, centered way. If we allow angry thoughts to enter our hearts, bitterness can set in and destroy our peace.

Our anger is often linked to impatience. Proverbs 16:32 makes it clear that God sees no value in uncontrolled anger or impatience. To become more like Jesus, we must practice both patience and self-control, especially in angry moments. I know this is easier said than done, but I also know it gets easier with practice. Bearing these fruits of the Spirit is far more valuable in God's eyes than venting our anger or winning an argument in a burst of impatience.

A person who lacks self-control is like a city with broken-down walls (Prov. 25:28). This powerful word picture shows us the state of our minds, hearts, and souls when we fail to apply self-control to our anger. Letting our angry thoughts simmer, leak out, or explode breaks down our walls of protection and gives the enemy easy access to build strongholds. Pray that God will help you control your anger so that your mind, heart, and soul are strong and healthy.

The Bible tells us that our mind will lead us either to death or life, depending on whether we let our sinful nature or the Holy Spirit control us (Rom. 8:6 NLT). We don't usually think in these black-and-white terms when it comes to anger. But God is telling us there are only two paths to choose, and we have control over which path we choose through our thought lives. Every morning, ask the Holy Spirit to take control of your thoughts, including your angry thoughts, and lead you on the path toward life. You will gain clarity into your thought-life problem with anger when you ask the Holy Spirit to control your mind.

God's grace transforms us so that we want to bear the fruit of self-control. His grace teaches us self-control while getting rid of our worldliness and ungodliness (Titus 2:11–12). Ask God to give you a fresh dose of grace each day. He will work his grace into your heart and mind, nurturing the fruit of self-control in your thought life.

I need grace and self-control in a particular area. I have a terrible habit of cursing, but only when I'm angry. Lately God has been convicting me of this sin, which I have not dealt with in a focused manner. I'm praying that God will give me more self-control when I'm tempted to curse in anger, because I don't want blessing and curses to keep pouring out of my mouth (James 3:7–10 NLT). This has been a foothold for the enemy for decades, and I'm starting to address it in earnest now. Maybe it's an area where you could benefit from self-control too.

I'm sure none of us would choose to be a slave to anger, though it has enslaved many of us for years (2 Pet. 2:19 NLT). If anger has too much power over you, meditate on the verses in this chapter daily for the next month. God will set you free from its power over your thought life and your heart. He will reap a harvest of self-control in you like never before.

MORE MEDITATION VERSES

- An angry person stirs up conflict, and a hot-tempered person commits many sins. (Prov. 29:22)

- I will not accuse them forever, nor will I always be angry, for then they would faint away because of me—the very people I have created. (Isa. 57:16)

- But God said to Jonah, "Is it right for you to be angry about the plant?" (Jon. 4:9a)

- Get rid of all bitterness, rage and anger, brawling and slander, along with every form of malice. (Eph. 4:31)

❧ Look after each other so that none of you fails to receive the grace of God. Watch out that no poisonous root of bitterness grows up to trouble you, corrupting many. (Heb. 12:15 NLT)

Prayer

Father in heaven,

I praise you for being slow to anger. You have every reason to be angry for the thousands of times I have disobeyed you. But you are full of mercy and grace toward your children, and I marvel at your willingness to overlook my sins for the sake of your Son, Jesus Christ.

I confess that angry thoughts have flared through my mind without examination or repentance. Sometimes I internalize anger that should be confronted. At other times I leak it out in sneaky ways, never directly dealing with the problem. Still other times, I explode and wound people with my words and actions. Some angry incidents are now lodged in my soul due to bitterness. I need your cleansing Spirit to wash away all the negative effects of anger from my heart.

Thank you for offering me hope of change, Jesus. Thank you for giving me examples in your Word of how to handle anger and how not to handle anger. I want to become more like you, acting in anger only when it is righteous and necessary.

Bear the fruit of self-control in my thought life and in my heart, Lord. The next time angry thoughts fly through my mind, help me stop and examine the root problem. Help me learn from my mistakes and begin to control my words and actions with the help of your Holy Spirit.

In Jesus's name,
Amen.

REFLECTION QUESTIONS

1. What is your most common anger style: repressing, leaking, or exploding? Why?

2. What is the most common feeling underlying your most frequent reason for anger? How will you handle it differently next time?

3. In which situation will you benefit most from the fruit of self-control?

NOTES

[1] June Hunt, "4 Sources of Angry Inferno in the Heart," *Christian Post*, October 9, 2013, https://www.christianpost.com/news/pub-wed-4-sources-of-angry-inferno-in-the-heart-106057/.

[2] Julie Clinton, *A Woman's Path to Emotional Freedom: God's Promise of Hope and Healing* (Eugene, OR: Harvest House, 2010), 58.

CHAPTER FIFTEEN

UNFORGIVING THOUGHTS

Bear with each other and forgive one another
if any of you has a grievance against someone.
Forgive as the Lord forgave you.

—COLOSSIANS 3:13

In a past season as a freelance writer, I served as a ghostwriter for professional blogs. Some of my blog posts were morally neutral assignments, like the ones I wrote for dentists, chiropractors, service contractors, or online teachers. Others were much harder to write, like posts for criminal defense attorneys. I feared that I would be indirectly helping a drug dealer or sex offender get a lighter sentence. Even though I knew it would make more sense to get those dreaded articles finished first, I often put them off to the end.

That's what I've done with this chapter on unforgiving thoughts. It's one of the hardest to write, but it's probably the one I need the most. Maybe you do too. And it's where God can truly transform our thinking through Christian meditation.

One summer, when I was about eleven years old, I was alone with my dad's second wife. This was a rare occurrence—I'm guessing my younger sister was helping my dad with some task, and my youngest sister was napping. She and I were canning tomatoes and baking zucchini bread on a hot and humid August afternoon. A project-lover at heart, I was content to peel tomatoes, chop walnuts, and shred zucchini as long as we didn't have to talk. Even though my primary love language is quality time and conversation, this person was not on the top of my list for forming connection. I worked in silence for hours while my thought life hummed with activity.

As we worked in tandem, I couldn't turn my heart away from the parade of negative memories. They marched through my mind in chronological order. The night my dad didn't come home to us because he was with her. The day they got married, when everyone's eyes were on me and my sister as reluctant and heartbroken flower girls. The many times I heard mean things about her and experienced hard situations. It seemed like everyone in my family was set against her, including me.

For the first time, I didn't think she was all bad. She was just another mom canning the tomatoes from her garden, so she could make fresh-tasting spaghetti and chili all winter long. Food that would feed me too.

My parade of thoughts was based on unforgiveness. Even though I had learned about forgiveness in religion classes and church, I hadn't experienced it at home. We were all holding grudges against this woman, and it was hard to see why we should drop them. She would probably hurt us all again. As the water rose to a boil, I tamped down the parade of feelings while I wiped the rims of the canning jars clean. The feelings were simply too much for me to sort out as a girl ready to start seventh grade in a few weeks.

I didn't realize it then, but God planted a seed of compassion in my heart that day, like a tomato seed that slipped down into the dark space between the stove and cabinets. After many years, it received the light of God's love. I no longer have hard feelings toward her. I can even sincerely give her a hug and speak with her now, genuinely appreciative of who she is. The process of forgiving her took a very long time and a huge amount of thought-life transformation. If it's possible for me, it's possible for you too.

WHY FORGIVENESS IS SO HARD

Most of us have pockets of unforgiveness in our thought lives. It can be related to a family member, bully, friend, boyfriend, husband, child, boss, coworker, church leader, or a stranger. It can even be related to an entity like a school or company, or to God himself. Like Matthew West's truth-filled song says (oh, how often my local Christian radio station plays it right when I am struggling), forgiveness is one of those areas we'd rather avoid. Yet the lack of it exacts a heavy toll on our relationship with God and others.

Why is it so hard to forgive? Because it feels like letting someone off the hook. It's human nature to seek fairness, to level the scales when wrong occurs. You hit me; I hit you back. Then we're even, right? Not according to God. He wants us to take the highest road possible—not simply the high road of letting go—and pay others back with compassion and kindness when we feel hatred toward them for what they've done wrong. This requires a thought-life overhaul, because the enemy makes it all too easy to replay the grievances in succession, over and over, twenty-four hours a day.

"But you don't know my story," you say. All of us have one of those ace-in-the-hole stories of a person who wounded us or one of our loved ones big time, and I mean BIG time. I have an assortment of those stories, and I'll share one of them with you here.

I'm thinking of someone that my state declares to be subject to prison sentences for the harm they committed against my loved one. Yet this person may never receive a government-enforced consequence for their heinous actions. Forgiveness is not what naturally rises in me when I type out these words. A white-hot substance known as vengeance boils up from a hidden volcano of unforgiveness in my mind. When this volcano erupts, the enemy throws a party complete with confetti and chocolate cake to keep me coming back for more.

Jesus is standing in my mind's battlefield right now, acknowledging the burning lava around my feet that threatens to scorch and scar me. He is not asking me to hide the lava or pretend it's not there. He is standing in front of me with special heavenly tools to clean it up and take it away, but only if I give him permission.

"Why," I ask, "do you want this mess?"

He looks me in the eyes and says, "The real question is, why do you want to hold onto it?"

I feel the heat radiating upward around my ankles. He is giving me a choice I don't deserve. I know he is the only one able to perfectly deliver justice.

Tears well up in my eyes. "Take it, Jesus," I say. "I can't handle it anyway. It's killing me."

He uses his supernaturally strong tools to scoop it up into an impermeable container while smiling broadly at me. "I'm proud of you," he says. "You were never intended to manage it. Let me take care of it, beloved."

It takes faith to believe that God can handle vengeance better than you. Forgiveness *is* letting your offender off a hook. But it is also putting them onto God's hook and walking away in peace, trusting him to perfectly dole out justice according to his omniscience. And trusting him to give pure mercy if he so chooses.

There's another tricky twist to forgiveness that makes it so tough. Deborah Smith Pegues writes, "I believe when we have been damaged, deprived, or disadvantaged by another, we instinctively want to be compensated for our loss."[1] We want an apology, refund, or reward that we may never receive this side of heaven. Forgiveness is satisfaction with receiving God himself rather than our offender's restitution.

Unforgiveness can be a major block in our relationship with God. R. T. Kendall writes in *Total Forgiveness*:

> When Jesus said, "If you forgive men when they sin against you, your heavenly Father will also forgive you," He was not talking about how to achieve salvation. He was referring to receiving the anointing of God and participating in an intimate relationship with the Father. Unless we are walking in a state of forgiveness toward others, we cannot be in an intimate relationship with God.[2]

Next time you read Matthew 6:14–15, look at it through the lens of this quote. Remember that the quality of your relationship with God is intricately linked to the level of unforgiveness lava in your heart. Let Jesus clean it out for you, so you can walk in peace with him.

HOW MEDITATION HELPS YOU WITH FORGIVENESS

Perhaps no other area of our thought life will benefit more from a repeated focus on God's Word than forgiveness. It is a process that doesn't happen overnight, but with regular effort, forgiveness can become a way of life just like meditation.

First, you must admit that you have unforgiveness toward someone. Meditate on Psalm 19:12 to locate unforgiveness in your heart. Ask God to reveal your lava-laden places and how they are harming you. When he reveals them, ask him to clean them up for you.

Consider the sins you've committed in the past. Think about the ways God has forgiven you for your sins. Meditate on how joyful you feel when God washes away one of your terrible sins (Ps. 32:1 NLT). You can experience relief, joy, and peace when you release someone else through forgiveness.

God puts our sins far out of sight, much farther than the eye can see. The Bible says he places our sins as far away as the east and west are from each other (Ps. 103:12). He wants us to get to the point where we can put the offenses of others far away too. I don't believe God asks us to forget those wrongs, because they are part of our stories that he can use for good. Yet he wants us to release the power those wrongs have over us and let them rest in the past.

Jesus modeled forgiveness, even in his most painful moments. The Roman soldiers had no regard for Jesus's holiness when they nailed him to the cross, spit on him, mocked him, placed a crown of thorns on his head, and wagered for his clothing. In his excruciating and undeserved pain, he asked God to forgive them (Luke 23:34). We should strive to forgive others even as they are enacting sins upon us, just as Jesus did.

To take the highest road I mentioned before, we can't simply check forgiveness off a "one and done" list. As Christ followers, we must go above and beyond what the culture deems as fair, forgiving many times over. Peter thought that forgiving seven times was more than generous, but Jesus pressed him to forgive far more (Matt. 18:21–22). Jesus challenges us to keep forgiving so bitterness doesn't invade our hearts. We must model our forgiveness on God's patient and perfect will rather than common practice.

A lightning-bolt verse of Scripture like Mark 11:25 reminds us how important forgiveness is to God. He encourages us to wait to commune with him until we forgive someone else. This verse isn't a threat of punishment; it's an invitation to a highest-road faith. If you come upon a grudge while you are praying, be sure to lay it out before God. He will help strengthen your faith if you make forgiveness a high priority.

Bearing with one another means we're in it for the long haul (Col. 3:13). Long-haul relationships require forgiveness. We don't simply drop the relationship (unless abuse is occurring). In most relationships, we're called to keep on forgiving rather than fleeing in self-protection. Forgiveness is the oil in the engine of human relationships, and God has tucked away a limitless supply of that oil in your prayer and meditation closet.

PURSUING COMPASSION

One of the guideposts on the highest road of forgiveness is showing compassion to your offender. Compassion requires you to slow down, take deep breaths, and do some research into the reasons your offender acted the way he or she did. Your offender probably acted from a position of hurt. Compassion doesn't excuse their behavior, but it can broaden your understanding and cool the lava flow in your thought life.

Do you have a black sheep in your family? Someone who stains the family's reputation and makes forgiveness an enormous challenge? The black sheep in my family has made many poor choices. This sheep has stirred our family's hurt, fear, frustration, and injustice for decades. I know the black sheep's awful background story, and I understand why this sheep stays in a flock of other black sheep rather than rejoining the family flock. Yet I've hardened my heart against the pain, like many others in my family have done.

One summer we held a joyful family celebration in the city park to celebrate a homecoming. The all-American event turned into a disaster when the black sheep showed up. This broken, hurting sheep caused such a raucous scene that we had to call the police. Our family had seen many black sheep spectacles over the years, but this one topped the Most Embarrassing list. We shook our heads in exasperation as the black sheep rode away in a police car.

After that day, the black sheep suddenly stopped working for an older brother. This put the older brother in a financial bind, and the family didn't blame him for being at his wits' end. We weren't quite sure what happened to the black sheep, and we didn't know what to expect at Thanksgiving.

When the black sheep stood at the doorway of my grandparents' home that November, the older brother walked straight toward him. I watched in dread, fearing another chaotic scene. But the older brother approached the black sheep with outstretched arms. He welcomed the sheep back into the family flock with compassion, demonstrating to the rest of us that forgiveness was the best solution.

That scene replays in my mind when I have trouble forgiving someone. Even if someone has hurt you for years, has no intention of changing, and may not be sorry for what they have done, you can forgive them in a spirit of compassion. You don't have to reconcile or even speak to the person to show compassion. You can offer it as a behind-the-scenes gift, based on understanding and humility. By studying Scripture and following God's example, you can offer compassion to your offender.

Compassion is an important part of the Christian life. It is even listed as one of the valuable virtues in 1 Peter 3:8. Let's look at each virtue and how it relates to compassion.

Finally, all of you, be like-minded,

This verse doesn't mean we should be caught up in groupthink. It means that we can show compassion by stepping in the other person's shoes and understanding her viewpoint. Stepping into another's world is a vital part of showing compassion.

be sympathetic,

When we show sympathy to others, we validate their feelings. Sympathy does not mean that you have walked their same paths. But it does mean that you can look at their paths, acknowledge the difficulties, and cut them some slack. Your sympathy toward others is an expression of kindness.

love one another,

God tells us in Proverbs 10:12 that love covers all wrongs. When we look at someone through the lenses of love, compassion naturally results. It takes a little effort to put on those love glasses, but they can make all the difference in how we relate to our offenders.

be compassionate and humble.

Along with compassion, we must show humility. This virtue acknowledges that we are sinful beings, just as our offenders are. We will commit sins of commission and omission as they do. Our humility helps us stand alongside our offenders, instead of distancing ourselves from them or looking down upon them.

God does not withhold compassion from any single person. He offers it even to those who will never accept him as long as they draw breath (Ps. 145:9). You are also called to offer forgiveness and compassion to everyone who hurts you—no exceptions.

Understanding this truth about God can help you realize the priority compassion must have in your thought life.

Like forgiveness, compassion is available to us because God first offered it to us as his followers. God has the right to be angry with us for our sins, but chooses to show us mercy and compassion instead (Deut. 13:17). When you meditate on the Lord's gift of compassion, you catch a glimpse of God's majesty compared with your lowliness. The closer you get to God, the more you want to be like Jesus. He will help you offer compassion to your offender.

God offers us compassion again and again, not just once. He keeps delivering us from our sins when we cry out to him, and he shows us compassion each time he rescues us (Neh. 9:28). When we forgive seventy-seven times rather than only seven times, we must offer compassion that many times as well. This takes time and practice. The more often you think of your offender with compassion rather than bitterness, the easier it will be to offer compassion.

God shows his compassion within a close, loving relationship. He is compassionate like a father is with a young child who has made a mistake (Ps. 103:13). Whenever that is possible for you, that's the route you should take with others. If that isn't possible, you can still offer compassion from a loving stance in your heart rather than staying entrenched in a call for vengeance.

Do your sins feel like stains? Do others' sins feel like stains on your heart? Just as God blots out a stain of sin, we can blot out a grudge with the cleansing power of God's love (Ps. 51:1). As we let his love flow through us to a hurtful person, we can remove the stains of their sins with compassion.

Compassion offers comfort and joy for you as the giver. Even if a renewed relationship is not possible with your offender, you receive these blessings by offering compassion. Comfort and joy work together to bring peace to your thought life. You can

celebrate God's compassion through joyful singing in your meditation time (Isa. 49:13).

Jesus offered compassion and healing in close proximity,
not from a distance. He touched the eyes of two blind men who
needed his miraculous healing and compassion (Matt. 20:34). As
often as possible, offer your compassion closely too. A face-to-face
meeting, phone call, or a card can transform a relationship marred
by unforgiveness.

Tuck Ephesians 4:32 into your mental filing cabinet through
regular meditation. Pull it out every time the hot lava starts to
bubble and flow. Ignore the enemy as he attempts to set up tables
for another unforgiveness party. Think about Jesus offering to take
your mess and how you can offer forgiveness and compassion to
your offender.

▬▬▬▬▬ MORE MEDITATION VERSES ▬▬▬▬▬

∿ But you, Lord, are a compassionate and gracious
God, slow to anger, abounding in love and faithfulness. (Ps. 86:15)

∿ Your compassion, LORD, is great; preserve my life
according to your laws. (Ps. 119:156)

∿ If you, LORD, kept a record of sins, Lord, who could
stand? But with you there is forgiveness, so that we
can, with reverence, serve you. (Ps. 130:3–4)

∿ Once again you will have compassion on us. You
will trample our sins under your feet and throw
them into the depths of the ocean! (Mic. 7:19 NLT)

∿ Forgive us our sins, as we have forgiven those who
sin against us. (Matt. 6:12 NLT)

❧ When [Jesus] saw the crowds, he had compassion
on them, because they were harassed and helpless,
like sheep without a shepherd (Matt. 9:36).

❧ "Blessed are those whose lawless deeds are forgiven,
and whose sins are covered" (Rom. 4:7 ESV).

Prayer

Father in heaven,

*I praise you for being compassionate and forgiving. If you with-
held these gifts from me, I would be doomed to destruction. You are
my perfect example of how to treat others, because you welcome me
into your arms despite the many ways I've hurt you.*

*I confess that pools of the lava of unforgiveness threaten to spring
up every time I think about certain people. You know the whole story,
Lord. You know the reasons for the wrongs that I can't understand,
and you are wise not to explain it all to me. I ask your forgiveness
for my unforgiveness, God. I don't want my unforgiveness lava to
damage me, my relationship with you, or my relationships with
others anymore.*

*Thank you for offering me a chance to take the highest road of
forgiveness for your glory, Jesus. Thank you for teaching me not only
to forgive once, but to keep forgiving. Thank you that I don't have to
generate forgiveness, compassion, or love by myself. You will supply
it for me as I walk closely with you.*

*Help me release the power that past offenses have on my life.
Help me know whether to go to my offenders and make things right
or simply settle the matter in my heart before your eyes. Remind me
of your example so I can continue to choose the highest road possible
in each situation. Keep my heart and mind on the obedient path of
continued forgiveness and compassion.*

In Jesus's name,
Amen.

REFLECTION QUESTIONS

1. When you read the story of hot lava, which person came to your mind?

2. What is Jesus telling you to do about an area of unforgiveness?

3. Which verse pinged your spirit most, and how does it inspire you to offer forgiveness or compassion to others?

NOTES

[1] Deborah Smith Pegues, *Forgive, Let Go, and Live* (Eugene, OR: Harvest House, 2015), 13.

[2] R. T. Kendall, *Total Forgiveness* (Lake Mary, FL: Charisma House, 2007), 87.

CHAPTER SIXTEEN

SELF-FOCUSED THOUGHTS

Turn my heart toward your statutes and
not toward selfish gain.

—PSALM 119:36

D o you love a narcissist? I do. Loving this person has taught me much about the extremes of self-focused thoughts and plenty about my own problem with selfishness.

I love someone who has been clinically diagnosed with narcissistic personality disorder. People with this disorder have normally been hurt so badly in the past that they work hard to preserve their meticulously constructed "perfect" masks.

When I'm around this person, I must measure every word before I speak it. Somehow, the conversations always center back on the person, no matter how personal the matter is to me. Any attempts to change the conversation to neutral territory are directed toward the insatiable vortex of self-aggrandizement. It's exhausting, and that's why I limit my time with this person, even though I will always love them from a distance.

In studying this person's toxic behavior patterns, it's tempting to point a "shame on you" or "don't you know better" finger of accusation. But the more I contemplate this person's actions, the more I see similar (yet more normal) threads of selfishness in my own thought life.

If I'm not careful, I can turn a simple misunderstanding into a personal attack. I can throw a big pity party in mere moments if I dwell on a certain thought too long. A holiday can turn into a hospital for my feelings alone, disregarding the needs and desires of others. Even though I'm not a narcissist, I do struggle with self-centered thoughts, just like every other human in history.

My past hurts, many of which I've mentioned in previous chapters, tempt me to feel sorry for myself. As a true victim of emotional abuse, I must choose daily to refuse the victim mentality. In the moments of abuse, a victim cannot be blamed for the harm happening to her. But once she has healed, she has the power to throw off the enemy's attacks and refuse to keep thinking like a victim. The victim mind-set infected me for decades, and I have overcome it only with the truth in God's Word. If you struggle with it yourself, you can find freedom in Christian meditation.

In this chapter, we'll focus more on the everyday variety of self-focused thoughts. Thoughts that protect our own interests when we have opportunities to serve. Thoughts that recall Eve's original temptation, when she could only see what she wanted instead of what God wanted for her. The truth of God's Word can inoculate us against the infection of self-focused thoughts, which run so rampant in our contemporary culture.

The Bible tells us that the closer we come to the time when Jesus returns, the more we will see people become "lovers of themselves" (2 Tim. 3:2). We will probably see greater temptations for self-focused thoughts in days to come. That's why practicing Christian meditation now will guard your heart and mind today and protect you in the future, keeping you close to God and the truth.

THE DEEP ROOTS OF SELF-FOCUSED THOUGHTS

We only need to turn to the first few pages of our Bibles to find the roots of self-focused thoughts. When Adam was created, he was given both dominion over the Garden of Eden and freedom to enjoy it. God gave him only one limit: "You must not eat from the tree of the knowledge of good and evil, for when you eat from it you will certainly die" (Gen. 2:16–17).

In the very next verse, God stated that it was not good (inside a perfect creation!) for Adam to be alone. So, he created Eve from one of Adam's ribs, and gave them both great blessings and peace.

The enemy approached Eve in snake form and questioned God's directive, planting seeds of doubt in her mind. She added to God's Word in Genesis 3:3, saying that God told them to not even touch it, though I'm sure touching the forbidden fruit wasn't a good idea anyway. Then the enemy directly contradicted God's Word, planting a king-size seed of selfishness in her mind: "you will be like God" if you eat the fruit.

What did Eve know about God? She knew him to be the creator and sustainer of all life. His power and majesty were ever present. His goodness and beauty constantly flowed. She walked in perfect communion with him. She saw a full-color picture of his righteous character.

Eve knew that God needed nothing. Creation depended on him, not the other way around. Though she had been created to be dependent on God and her husband, she saw the sheen of attraction on the idea of not needing anything, just like God. The shell on the seed of selfishness began to crack open.

She began rationalizing, and the seed sank into the soil of her thought life. Thoughts like these ran through her mind as she gazed at the fruit. *This fruit is good for food. How bad can it be? It's perfectly ripe, so it must be sweeter than anything I've ever tasted. It's set apart from all the other fruits because it will grant me special wisdom. I'll just handle it for a minute. Oh, it's beautiful. A little bite won't matter.*

She forgot that God sees everything, even single nips of selfishness. She forgot God completely as the fruit touched her lips and tongue. Eve was the first human to taste the fruit of self-focused thoughts.

Adam didn't stop her, even though he was right there with her. He accepted the fruit she gave him. But as they looked into each other's eyes, with the sweet taste still in their mouths, shame filled them for the first time. Division, fear, blame, pain, curses, and suffering soon followed. Because Eve allowed those self-focused thoughts to take root, all of us have suffered ever since.

In his best-selling book *The Purpose Driven Life*, Rick Warren opens with this sentence: "It's not about you."[1] Why? Because we will always be drawn to thinking that life is all about us. We have all made bad choices of rationalizing, second-guessing God's laws, and forgetting that he's always present, watching over us with love. Each one of our sins has pride at its root, because our sinful nature will always believe that we know better than God, and we don't want to be dependent on anyone or anything else.

Selfishness, pride, arrogance, and haughtiness are roundly condemned in Scripture. Consider what God has to say about selfishness, and use Scripture to confess your wrongs and choose a better path.

God does not welcome arrogant people into his presence, because they arouse his anger in their refusal to admit fault (Ps. 5:5). Arrogant people can expect to receive rebuke (Ps. 119:21) and punishment (Prov. 16:5). God stores up his anger for those who live only for themselves (Rom. 2:8). If we don't rid our mind's battlefield of self-focused thoughts, these are the tough consequences that await us.

God takes our self-focused thoughts personally. He will not share his glory with anyone; he alone deserves to be exalted (Isa. 2:11). The more blessings we have, the more we will be tempted to become self-focused and turn away from him (Ezek. 28:5, Hosea 13:6). God knows that a prideful woman has no room in her thoughts for him (Ps. 10:4). He will not put up with a proud heart (Ps. 101:5); he promises that pride will have a humiliating ending (Prov. 16:18). Any time we put on a spirit of pride or arrogance, we are setting ourselves up for a painful lesson.

ERADICATING SELF-FOCUSED THOUGHTS THROUGH MEDITATION

I enjoy gardening, but it requires a constant battle against weeds. If I'm not vigilant, they will overtake my garden space and quickly choke out the healthy plants.

Since I live in the woods, I have an extra-strong weed growing in my rock garden: poison ivy. Its roots go very deep, harkening back to the days when the property was completely covered in trees and vines. I can't simply pull it up or keep cutting it back. I must use strong chemical agents to eradicate poison ivy from places where it doesn't belong, since its roots are resistant to regular removal methods.

Self-focused thoughts are the same way. Since pride is attached to every sin we commit, we must double down on our efforts to eradicate the seeds and roots of self-focused thoughts from our mind. The enemy wants them to multiply and spread as far as possible, forming a poisonous carpet at the basis of every thought. You need to pray for the Holy Spirit to help you recognize and remove the seeds of these thoughts before they take root, and help you pull up old roots that just won't quit producing vines.

> *No discipline seems pleasant at the time, but painful. Later on, however, it produces a harvest of righteousness and peace for those who have been trained by it. (Heb. 12:11)*

Removing self-focused thoughts from our minds is a lot like receiving discipline. No one enjoys being called out for doing things wrong. But as we clear those noxious weeds from our minds, we grant more growing space for peace and righteousness— virtues all of us want to harvest.

> *[Love] does not dishonor others, it is not self-seeking, it is not easily angered, it keeps no record of wrongs. (1 Cor. 13:5)*

True love doesn't seek its own satisfaction. It is kind, gentle, forgiving, and compassionate to others rather than self-protective. Study the roots on one of the love plants in your mind. Ask God to show you if any self-seeking motives are attached, and if they are, ask for his help in removing them.

> *Turn my heart toward your statutes and not toward selfish gain. (Ps. 119:36)*

God's Word is a preventive treatment against self-focused thoughts. It is like a spray that combats weed seeds before they ever sprout. The more we meditate on his laws, the more he will dig up the old roots of pride and prevent other pride seeds from sprouting.

Where there is strife, there is pride,
but wisdom is found in those who take advice. (Prov. 13:10)

Strife is like a storm that beats down the good plants in our hearts. It batters and weakens them. When we eliminate pride, we stop the storms we have induced in our own hearts. By choosing to eradicate self-focused thoughts from our thought life through Christian meditation, we will gain wisdom that will calm the strife levels rooted in arrogance.

PURSUING HUMILITY

Humility is like fertilizer for all the healthy thoughts in our minds. In John 15, Jesus tells us that he is the vine and we are the branches; we are to abide in him to bear much fruit. We cannot abide in him unless we take on a humble, dependent spirit. He wants to reverse the curse Eve received in the garden and plant a new garden in us. But it cannot thrive unless we have a humble spirit which admits that apart from Jesus, we can do nothing (John 15:5).

Humility strengthens our minds with wisdom (Prov. 11:2), which helps us become better caretakers of our thought lives. We will have increased ability to weed out self-focused thoughts when we take a humble position toward God and others. Humility brings us honor before God and other people (Prov. 29:23 NLT).

Humility differs from humiliation, because God values humility but uses humiliation as a consequence for bad behavior. He opposes those who are proud but opens his arms in grace to the humble (James 4:6). Even though our culture values pride over humility, God elevates the humble. Jesus himself was the humblest person who ever lived, yet he is also the King of kings. We can follow his example to form a countercultural pathway in our thought lives.

Beth Moore writes, "Humility is the heart of the great paradox: we find our lives when we lose them to something much larger."[2] God gives grace freely to us when we decide to give our selfishness over to him. He will not resist us; he will give us his best when we desire humility more than pride.

In a culture full of self-promotion and show-offs, the Holy Spirit is actively seeking those who have the attitude expressed in Psalm 131. He loves taking up residence in believers who are humble and who value God's virtues more than the world's shiny offerings. Our materialistic culture constantly appeals to our self-focused nature. We must fight it through meditation on verses like Proverbs 16:19, especially in those moments when we stare at a piece of "fruit" and begin rationalizing why it would be good for us to eat.

Romans 12:16 is a pH test for the soil in your mind. Do you enjoy the company of regular people? If so, the pH level in your mind is balanced, meaning that good relationships can grow there. Too acidic with disharmony or too alkaline with conceit, and healthy relationships can't grow. There is no room for boasting to grow in a healthy mind garden. When you are tempted to boast about anything, meditate on 1 Corinthians 13:4 and scatter some humility in your thought life. Use the fertilizer of humility to correct the soil and watch your relationships flourish.

God promises great rewards for those with a humble spirit (Prov. 22:4). Everything we think, say, or do should be tinged with humility rather than a self-focused attitude. We show our humility best in relationships to others (Phil. 2:3). God is pleased when we honor him and others with a humble spirit. Keep pulling up self-focused thoughts and sprinkling humility in your thought life, and you will be living life according to God's will.

MORE MEDITATION VERSES

⌇ But when [King Nebuchadnezzar's] heart became arrogant and hardened with pride, he was deposed from his royal throne and stripped of his glory. (Dan. 5:20)

⌇ An unfriendly person pursues selfish ends and against all sound judgment starts quarrels. (Prov. 18:1)

⌇ Mockers are proud and haughty; they act with boundless arrogance. (Prov. 21:24 NLT)

⌇ A fool's proud talk becomes a rod that beats him, but the words of the wise keep them safe. (Prov. 14:3 NLT)

⌇ Fear of the LORD teaches wisdom; humility precedes honor. (Prov. 15:33 NLT)

⌇ But if you harbor bitter envy and selfish ambition in your hearts, do not boast about it or deny the truth. (James 3:14)

⌇ For where you have envy and selfish ambition, there you find disorder and every evil practice. (James 3:16)

⌇ As it is, you boast in your arrogance. All such boasting is evil. (James 4:16 ESV)

⌇ All of you, clothe yourselves with humility toward one another, because, "God opposes the proud but shows favor to the humble." (1 Pet. 5:5b)

Prayer

Father in heaven,

I praise you for choosing to stoop in humility to relate to me. Jesus, you didn't have to leave your throne of glory to save me. But you chose to do so with the most beautiful, humble spirit, and I am in awe of your total lack of selfishness.

I confess that selfishness is a daily battle for me. Pride is at the root of all my sinful thoughts and actions. I consistently choose what I want over what you want for me. I have fallen prey to the lie that I don't need you and that I know better than you what is good for me. Every day I struggle, but I want to repent of my selfish attitudes and keep growing in humility.

Thank you for showing me how valuable humility is to you. Jesus, thank you for modeling humility through many examples in your gospel. Your humility is perfect, inspiring, and so different from how I normally act. But I am grateful that you provide a path for me to follow.

I ask that you help me pull up and destroy the roots of self-focus in my thought life, Lord. Help me identify areas I have ignored or have never recognized before. As I meditate on your Word, make me a humbler follower of you. Give me courage to pursue your holy will in a culture that values pride over humility.

In Jesus's name,
Amen.

REFLECTION QUESTIONS

1. What new concept did you learn about self-focused thoughts from Eve's story? How can you apply it to your thought life?

2. Regarding your area of biggest struggle with self-focused thoughts, what actions can you take to keep them out of your thought life or pull up their roots?

3. In what relationship could you reap the biggest harvest from pursuing humility this week?

NOTES

[1] Rick Warren, *The Purpose Driven Life: What on Earth Am I Here For?* (Grand Rapids: Zondervan, 2002), 17.

[2] Beth Moore, *So Long, Insecurity: You've Been a Bad Friend to Us* (Carol Stream, IL: Tyndale House, 2010), 104.

CHAPTER SEVENTEEN

UNTRUE THOUGHTS

*Finally, brothers and sisters, whatever is true,
whatever is noble, whatever is right, whatever
is pure, whatever is lovely, whatever is admirable—if
anything is excellent or praiseworthy—think
about such things.*

—PHILIPPIANS 4:8

What's the main thing people have told you about yourself that you have a hard time believing to be true?

For me, it's "funny." My sense of humor is super dry, so not everyone appreciates it. But when a few people have told me in person, "You're funny," I always deflect it. Other people in my family are well known for being much funnier than me, so I think about them when people apply the funny label to me. It just doesn't seem to fit, though people keep telling me it's true. I'd rather believe the "you're not funny" lie about myself than accept the truth others tell me.

Maybe you have the opposite problem as well. Someone lied to you about who you are, and you decided to believe them. For decades, I believed the lie that I am lazy, because a few people insinuated that I didn't work hard enough. Then one, two, and eventually dozens of people told me I'm one of the hardest-working people they know, and I had to stack their evidence against the few lies a handful of people told me. I've started to believe the truth about myself: I'm rarely ever lazy.

I applied this truth last year when I went on a spiritual retreat. After breakfast I took a hike and enjoyed the woods, taking pictures of wildflowers and singing praises to God. But walking feels productive since I'm earning steps on my Fitbit. After my hike, my whole mind and body went into work mode against my will. But it was only 11:00 A.M. and I had the rest of the day to simply enjoy God's presence. Nothing to produce. I felt unsure of myself for the next few hours.

By 2:00 P.M. I had settled into God's perfect peace. I realized that I wasn't being lazy, but intentionally caring for my mind, heart, and soul by accepting rest. That weekend, God taught me I was a weary person who needed to come to him for rest. I had been denying the truth that I was overworked and worn to the bone, covering it up with extra work. But since the lies of those who said I was lazy played on repeat through my mind, I couldn't stop working hard enough to prove them wrong.

The only one who needs proof of who we are is God. Too many of us are living our lives according to untrue thoughts rather than truthful thoughts, trying to prove others wrong one way or another. Since the Garden of Eden, the enemy has been telling us lies to throw us off-balance. To make us question God's best.

Patsy Clairmont writes: "If we don't agree with what's true about ourselves, we don't change. It's that simple and that hard."[1] To live the life God wants us to live, we must agree with the truth and cast out the untruth, so God can change us into a likeness of Jesus. Living the Christian life isn't easy, but it is the only life worth living. God will help us transform our thought lives to recognize truths and untruths.

Essentially, every thought-life struggle described in this book is rooted in untruth. The enemy is the father of lies, accusing us with untruths every day. He tries to snare us with shades of the truth and even attempted to use the truth against Jesus when he was tempted. We must deliberately sidestep his untruths and choose God's truth in our thought lives through Christian meditation.

THE PROBLEM OF DECEIT

The enemy will try to deceive you in every possible way. He will take a good thought and twist the truth, or he will plant a bald-faced lie in your mind and see if you'll accept it. He will try to get you to question if God's Word is in your best interest. He attempts to match God's voice, so you question if you're hearing from God or the enemy. Remember, he used these tactics on Jesus himself (see Luke 4), so we will not be immune to these same spiritual warfare strategies.

All the lies serve to elevate the enemy above God, which has been his grand scheme since the beginning. He was once one of God's holy angels, but rebelled against God in his quest for ultimate power. He took many of heaven's angels with him, so he has millions of evil spirits at his command who work hard to support his deceitful campaigns. The enemy even disguises himself as an angel of light to try to deceive you in spiritual matters. His tactics are vicious, cruel, and always tainted with lies. We must study his tactics of deceit to remove untrue thoughts from our mind's battlefield.

Even if you keep your mind free from lies, you will need to guard closely against the lies of certain people who surround you (Jer. 9:4–6). The enemy is working hard to deceive as many people as possible, and you must depend on God's guidance and wisdom to know who is trustworthy and righteous. You can look for evidence like a love for God's Word, a humble spirit, and spiritual fruit in their lives. But you must guard your thought life against the influence of deceitful people as well as the deceiver himself.

There's one area where the enemy would love to deceive you most, and that's in leading you to believe that someone besides Jesus Christ is your Savior. Many will serve as false teachers who try to lead you away from the truth of God's Word (Matt. 24:4–5). As you meditate on God's Word, you will become familiar with God's voice, character, and teachings. You will be more likely to recognize an impostor when he or she appears as you steep yourself in the truth.

Self-deception is a constant threat in our sinful nature (Gal. 6:3). We must constantly guard against self-deceit through regular prayer, confession, study, and meditation. It's also important to meet with other believers in corporate worship and small groups to retain a humble and dependent spirit. Otherwise, each one of us can fall into the trap of self-focused thoughts.

God wants us to apply his Word so it changes our hearts and minds, not simply to allow it to flow in and out of our consciousness. A committed believer accepts the entire Word of God as truth and applies all its laws and principles to daily living (James 1:22). You can do this by asking yourself every time you meditate, "How can I apply this verse to my daily life?"

We will deal with the deceiver as long as we are breathing on this earth. But God has the final victory already secured (Rev.

20:10). Once the enemy is cast into the lake of torment, he can never cross over and deceive us again (see Luke 16:19–31). This is a verse you can use for meditation and praise after you have suffered a spiritual attack.

ACCEPTING TRUTH THROUGH MEDITATION

Henry Cloud and John Townsend say, "Like anything else from God, truth works *for* us, not *against* us."[2] The truth God wants us to accept can revolutionize our thinking. We can internalize the truth by meditating on verses of truth.

In John 8:32, Jesus said that the truth will set us free. We all want the truth to set us free. The second sentence in this verse is often quoted, even in secular examples. But the truth is directly dependent on holding to Jesus's teachings, which are the actual, unbiased truth about life. There is no truth outside of what God says. He is the ultimate source of truth.

We need the Holy Spirit's help to determine the truth about ourselves: Are we living in any type of spiritual darkness? If so, we aren't really fellowshipping with God (1 John 1:6). We can call ourselves Christians, but if we are not living the Christian life as described in God's Word, we are deceiving ourselves. Any time we believe untrue thoughts, we fall captive to the enemy, who loves lies (John 8:44). We must align ourselves with God's truth to stay close to the Father of truth instead.

Do you always want to be right? I've fallen into this trap before. When I feel that desire to be right flaring up inside me, I gain humility through 1 John 1:8. I am a sinful being and will always struggle with sin. But I want to pursue the truth about myself so I can be more like Jesus, and this verse keeps me in check.

As we've seen throughout this book, God knows that we love truth when we obey him. Our obedience is a sure sign that we honor the truth and want to live in it. Regularly meditate on the

Ten Commandments and other laws God gave us, asking him to show you if you are disobeying any of them and choosing to believe lies instead of the truth (1 John 2:4).

You can receive both clarity and comfort through 1 John 3:19–20 when you're not sure if you have been deceived. Acknowledge God as knowing everything about you, including whether you have believed untrue thoughts. He will show you the truth and give you rest and peace in his presence.

MEDITATING ON THE TRUTH

As we wrap up our study of Christian meditation, we will consider Philippians 4:8, a powerful verse of Scripture for thought-life transformation. Paul encourages us to fix our minds on what pleases God, focusing on different aspects of truth. We will look at each virtue in our final review.

Finally, brothers and sisters, whatever is true,

Take each thought captive and examine it closely. Does it align with everything you know to be true about God? You can only know this if you regularly study and meditate on God's Word, exposing yourself to the greatest truth ever known. Remember that Jesus only speaks the truth, and listen for his still, small voice to determine whether your thoughts are based on the truth. Thinking about what is true can help you with anxious thoughts, as you consider whether your anxiety is based on truth or lies. It can also help you discover the factors underneath angry thoughts, so you can discover the truth about your responses.

whatever is noble

Noble thoughts are refined, respectful, and always in another person's best interest. Noble thoughts require courage to rise above difficult circumstances. They are forward-focused and brave. They can help you with defeated thoughts, because they inspire confidence in God. They can also help you overcome fearful thoughts as you use courage to fight your thought-life battles.

whatever is right

We know from meditating on the verses of Scripture in this book that God wants us to love his laws. He longs for us to live a righteous life of obedience, which reflects our love for him. Thinking about what is right helps us straighten out our careless thoughts with the righteousness of intention. Right thoughts also help us choose freedom in Christ instead of getting stuck in guilt.

whatever is pure

Pure thoughts cleanse our mind of the foreign concepts that push us away from God. They help us worship and revere God's holiness and inspire us to live more godly lives. Impure and idolatrous thoughts are cancelled out by thinking about what is pure in God's Word.

whatever is lovely

No matter how difficult life becomes, we can always choose to praise God for his beautiful attributes. We can praise him for giving us life, for the overwhelming beauty in his creation, and for the opportunities he gives us every day to learn something new. Thinking about what is lovely helps us overcome negative and painful thinking.

whatever is admirable

Admirable thoughts look for the best in others. We can learn much about Christian living through studying the lives of other believers. Admirable thoughts help reverse our thoughts that criticize others. When we choose to look at what is admirable in ourselves as beloved children of God, these thoughts can also help us overcome self-criticism.

—if anything is excellent

Focusing on what is excellent helps us seek out top-quality thoughts that please God. We can focus on what's best about a situation by choosing compassion over unforgiveness. We can also choose Jesus's excellent example of humility in our quest to destroy self-focused thoughts.

or praiseworthy—

As with lovely thoughts, we can always find reasons to give God praise based on who he is and what he does for us. Choosing to think about what is praiseworthy will help us set aside discontent and regretful thoughts. We can find many reasons to praise God when we focus on contentment and hope.

think about such things.

I hope this book has inspired you to take your thoughts captive (2 Cor. 10:5), put on the mind of Christ (1 Cor. 2:16), and be transformed by the renewing of your mind (Rom. 12:2). I pray that your mind is newly set on things above, rather than earthly things (Col. 3:2). Most of all, I pray this book inspires you to "Love the Lord your God with all your heart and with all your soul and with all your mind" (Matt. 22:37).

May your thought life be permanently transformed through the power of Christian meditation.

MORE MEDITATION VERSES

❧ Yet it is also new. Jesus lived the truth of this commandment, and you also are living it. For the darkness is disappearing, and the true light is already shining. (1 John 2:8 NLT)

- ∿ But we belong to God, and those who know God listen to us. If they do not belong to God, they do not listen to us. That is how we know if someone has the Spirit of truth or the spirit of deception. (1 John 4:6 NLT)

- ∿ And Jesus Christ was revealed as God's Son by his baptism in water and by shedding his blood on the cross—not by water only, but by water and blood. And the Spirit, who is truth, confirms it with his testimony. (1 John 5:6 NLT)

Prayer

Father in heaven,

I praise you for being the source of truth. No lies are found in you. You are completely trustworthy because the truth always shines in you. Your truth lights my path and clarifies my thinking.

I confess that I have often chosen to believe untruths about you, myself, and others. I have been deceived by the enemy and I have been deceived by others. The lies I've believed have distanced me from you, caused confusion in my mind, and brought suffering into my relationships. I am tired of giving the enemy control over my thought life, and I surrender it to you today.

Thank you for helping me transform my thoughts, Lord. Thank you for giving me so many examples in Scripture of ways I can focus on what's good instead of what's bad. Thank you for offering me newness of life and spiritual maturity when I pursue your truth.

Teach me to meditate on your Word every day for a new intake of truth. Help me to recognize untruths before they take root in my thinking. Protect me from the enemy's attacks and help me to put on godly thinking each day.

In Jesus's name,
Amen.

REFLECTION QUESTIONS

1. What untruths are you believing about yourself, based on what others have said?

2. What lies has the enemy deceived you into believing?

3. In what ways can meditating on Philippians 4:8 help you transform your thought life?

NOTES

[1] Patsy Clairmont, *Stained Glass Hearts: Seeing Life from a Broken Perspective* (Nashville: Thomas Nelson, 2011), 21.

[2] Henry Cloud and John Townsend, *How People Grow: What the Bible Reveals about Personal Growth* (Grand Rapids: Zondervan, 2001), 318.

ABOUT THE AUTHOR

Sarah Geringer is an author, speaker, and graphic designer. She is a member of the writing and proofreading team for the Proverbs 31 Ministries' *Encouragement for Today* devotions. Sarah is also a regular contributor to the *Hope-Full Living* devotionals and several faith-based websites, including A Wife Like Me, Devotable, and Woman to Woman Ministries. Her writing has been featured on the (in)courage blog and on LifeLetter Café Lifelines. She was the first-place winner in Kelly Balarie's Fear Fighting Writers Contest in March 2017 and the first-place winner in the poetry division at the 2017 All Write Now! Conference.

Sarah holds a bachelor of arts in English from Covenant College and a bachelor of fine arts in graphic design and illustration from Southeast Missouri State University. She lives in southeast Missouri with her husband and three children. You can follow Sarah as she writes about finding peace in God's Word at sarahgeringer.com.